DISAPPOINTMENTS

DISAPPOINTMENTS

*Books Not
Written,
Promise Not
Realized,
Dreams...*

JOHN E. BEERBOWER

P.J. Bear

"The fate of this man or that man was less than a drop,
although it was a sparkling one,
in the great blue motion of the sunlit sea."

T. H. White
The Once and Future King (1958)
Kindle Edition (2021), p.825.

CONTENTS

PREFACE

Disappointment. It comes in all shapes and sizes. Sometimes, we see it coming, or, even invite it; sometimes, it takes us by surprise. It can be a shock or a relief. So, that is my theme for this tiny volume.

I am still wandering.

It is easy to criticize. It is relatively easy to edit, revise and improve. The hard thing is to create from "scratch," to confront and overcome the blank page. Or, so it seems to me.

I had a knack for identifying and imagining ways to improve someone else's creation, whether it be a book, a play, a movie, a speech or an architectural design. To extend, massage or respond to someone else's idea. But, I was deficient when it came to creating something from nothing. For example, despite my long interest in architecture, I could not design my dream house in a vacuum; but, show me someone else's design and I will enhance it. Give me an empty shell and I will renovate it. My creative powers require constraints, structure, a starting point.

I do wonder, however, if I have been seeing as a difference in kind something that is really a matter of degree. Are there people so endowed that they can create something out of nothing; or does everyone necessarily build on, extend, embellish or react to (bounce off of) the creations of others? I suspect that the latter is the case. So, I lack the imagination of some others, but that may be something that could have been addressed by training, experience or study. Too late now.

Any writer of nonfiction will look for an angle, a theme, a perspective, that will give his book a claim of originality, of making a contribution to our understanding. The quality and quantity of research and the sharpness of the analysis will determine the lasting scholarly value of the work, if any, but the author's slant or take on the subject will control its sales. Does it scratch a widely held itch? Flatter a current prejudice? Push today's hot button? These are the things that engender sales. A few such stories will be enlightening or inspiring, some will be interesting. Some will pander, some inflame and some will just be silly. Some themes have no legs, they go nowhere. Throughout my writings I have tested, and often challenged, authors' themes.

I offer little of my own. Let he who cannot do, criticize those who do.

A bit of science, some personal reflections, several book reviews and stuff about race and racism.

Not that I planned it so. I just followed in my reading what peeked my interest and wrote about my reactions. When I was ready to create this book, I used what I had accumulated. This is the result.

CHAPTER 1

Books Not Written

Most of us have read books, attended plays or watched movies that began powerfully, causing us to be excited with anticipation, only to be disappointed by what followed. Here's to the books not written.

I.

David Brooks
The Second Mountain
(2019).

I previously quoted some memorable passages from *The Second Mountain*. The book had much promise, but it fell short, in my opinion.

Brooks begins the introduction to the book setting out his theme. Here are the highlights:

> "Every once in a while, I meet a person who radiates joy. ... I often find that their life has what I think of as a two-mountain shape. They got out of school, began their career or started a family, and identified the mountain they thought they were

meant to climb.... . The goals on that first mountain are the normal goals that our culture endorses — to be a success, to be well thought of, to get invited into the right social circles, and to experience personal happiness. ... Then something happens.

...

"Some people get to the top of that first mountain, taste success, and find it ... unsatisfying. ...Other people get knocked off that mountain by some failure. ... For still others, something unexpected happens that knocks them crossways: the death of a child, a cancer scare, a struggle with addiction, some life-altering tragedy that was not part of the original plan. ... They are down in the valley of bewilderment or suffering."

...

"These seasons of suffering have a way of exposing the deepest parts of ourselves and reminding us that we're not the people we thought we were. ... There is another layer to them they have been neglecting, a substrate where the dark wounds, and most powerful yearnings live. ...Some shrivel in the face of this kind of suffering. They seem to get more afraid and more resentful. ... Their lives become smaller and lonelier.

...

"But for others, this valley is the making of them. The season of suffering interrupts the superficial flow of everyday life. They see deeper into themselves and realize that down in the substrate, flowing from all the tender places, there is a fundamental ability to care, a yearning to transcend the self and care for others."

Id., pp.xi--xiii.

Powerful. The metaphor is vivid and evocative. The language is typical Brooks—eloquent, moving, inspirational. One anticipates a profound discussion of discontent, lack of fulfillment, the search for meaning, the confrontation with failure or personal tragedy.

Instead, however, Brooks focuses on people he has encountered who already live on the "Second Mountain." They are admirable, live meaningful lives, deserve recognition; but, their stories offer little solace to or advice for those of us staggering through the valley. Moreover, the label "Second Mountain" does not really seem particularly meaningful without the "First Mountain."

I craved stories of those who stumbled and fell and found ways and the strength to get back up. I was disappointed.

II.

Isabel Wilkerson
Caste:
The Origins of Our Discontents
(2020, 2023).

It is very well written, quite vivid and engrossing. The stories she introduces in Part 1—the re-emergence in the Arctic of anthrax from the frozen carcasses of poisoned reindeer that began to defrost, the rapid spread of the Corona virus, silent earthquakes—are suggestive of important lessons, of insightful analogies, of game-changing analyzes, promising a fascinating adventure.

But, then she introduces "caste," a supposedly ubiquitous structural element of various societies including, notably, America. On its face, her theory of caste would seem not to reflect any of the interesting implications of her opening stories. Caste does not seem to have been just resurrected from dormancy, to be spreading virulently or to have crept unnoticed throughout society. In contrast, one might argue that racism is like the Arctic anthrax, that anti-immigration sentiments are like the Corona virus and that moral bankruptcy has slowly overwhelmed us like silent earthquakes. A missed opportunity to develop some meaningful observations about MAGA and Trumpism based on these gripping analogies.

Now, that would have been an interesting book.

Her theory of caste is contrived. The caste system in India is very different from racism in the United States (or Great Britain). There have been millions of oppressed people in both countries, and there are similarities in the methods and forms of exploitation and discrimination, just as there are similarities between behavior in these countries and the treatment of women in parts of the Middle East and Africa or the treatment of minority groups in parts of Asia and Northern Africa. Otherwise, the origins, history and structure are quite distinct. *See, e.g., id.,* p.68.

The comparison with Nazi Germany (*id.,* pp.78-88) is silly. The fact that some Nazi social planners looked to laws that had existed in various states in America designed to promote racial purity by outlawing interracial marriages and criminalizing interracial sex does not establish a common system. There is no American parallel to the Nazis' Final Solution. The observation that the Nazis concluded that the definitions of Negro in some states was too inclusive (like "a single drop of blood") for their purposes establishes nothing relevant and is obviously stressed in an effort to engender outrage and prejudice. Such "grandstanding" has no proper role in a scholarly study. (I discuss some other examples in a later essay).

"While the Nazis praised 'the American commitment to legislating racial purity,' they could not abide 'the unforgiving hardness under which "an

---

American man or woman who has even a drop of Negro blood in their veins" counted as blacks,' Whitman [Yale legal historian James Q. Whitman] wrote 'The one-drop rule was too harsh for the Nazis.'" *Id.*, p.88.

Wilkerson provides numerous gripping, powerful stories of horrific violence by whites against Blacks. They are stories that should be told and should be remembered, but they are not evidence supporting her thesis. Analyses of how such things could happen would be valuable, but they are not found here. She quotes characterizations and colorfully worded comments by historians and other writers. These are not evidence of anything other than the views of those quoted. The analysis of the elements ("pillars") of caste is, to me, rather obvious and repetitious.

She prompts readers to infer that the strikingly strange fact that mortality rates for white American men began to rise in the early 2020s was the consequence of the progress being made by Blacks.

"[S]tarting just before the turn of the twenty-first century, the death rates among middle-aged white Americans, ages forty-five to fifty-four, began to rise, as the least educated, in particular, succumbed to suicide, drug overdoses, and liver disease from alcohol abuse," *Id.*, p.179.

"In a psychic way, the people dying of despair could be said to be dying of the end of an illusion, an awakening to the holes in an article of faith that an inherited, unspoken superiority, a natural deservedness over subordinated castes, would assure their place in the hierarchy." *Id.*, p.181.

Why? What is the point?

If she wants to makes such a claim, she should do so and attempt to demonstrate it.

Wilkerson observers that demographic trends in the United States indicate that in the next 20 years the "white population" will become the minority. This prospect has supposedly caused a panicked response from the dominant caste causing the War on Drugs, bans on abortion, efforts to curtail immigration and discrimination against LGBTQ citizens.

"Mass incarceration for nonviolent crimes, often on charges for which the dominant caste receives lesser sentences, keeps a disproportionate share of black men from the reproductive pool for long periods of time." *Id.*, p.393.

"All of these factors, undergirded by caste, keep the black birth rate structurally under assault." *Id.*, p.394.

Really?

Does anyone actually believe that the disproportionate (based on population) incarceration of Black men is part of a scheme, or is motivated by a desire, to reduce the Black birthrate? Do you?

And, how can restrictions on abortion, disproportionately occurring among Black woman, be intended to decrease the birthrate among Blacks?

Wilkerson recognizes the illogic and offers an "explanation":

"Bans on abortion would seem to open the door to a disproportionate number of black and brown births, but the caste system, throughout our history, has shown that it can mutate to sustain itself when under threat.

"...[S]ome Latinos, the white-adjacent middle-caste sub-groups already being courted by conservative elites, could conceivably be folded into the white population to shore up dominant caste power, as with the Italians and Irish in previous generations."

Id., pp.392-3.

And, incredibly, "forced reproduction suggests an underlying will to curate the American population to forestall the day that the dominant caste might be in the minority... ." *Id.*, p.395.

So, the nefarious plan is to ban abortion, increasing the Black birthrate, but offseting that by making certain Latinos "white," while reducing immigration of Latinos and restricting gay marriages. The grand plan to preserve the white majority. This may seem delusional; but, instead, it is just deceitful. The issue is not about caste or a white majority; it is about partisan politics: it is about the supposed efforts "to enshrine the objectives of a conservative minority..." (*id.*, p.392).

"Thus, with the caste system under threat, we are witnessing desperate efforts to impose the will of a dwindling but powerful subset of Americans onto the rest of the country." *Id.*, p.392.

Finally, notice her subtitle: "Origins of Our Discontent." Whose discontent? And, of what does it consist? We need to know before we can identify the origins. The "discontent" seems to be rather mercenary, actually, and its origin covetousness.

In the end, this is a remarkably unsatisfying and unsatisfactory book.

III.

"[A] story of economics, politics, and laws
that sowed the seeds of injustice
into the soil of the American economy."

...

"There are certainly stories of inspiration
to be found, but the overemphasis on
Horatio Alger tales of success can lead
to distraction."

Mehrsa Baradaran
The Color of Money:
Black Banks and the Racial Wealth Gap
(2017), p.7.

This book is quite frustrating. It could have told one or both of two important stories: one of the economic, political and legal forces that impeded Black economic progress and/or one of the heroic struggles of Blacks to get ahead. Neither quite makes it. The reasons are suggested by the quotations above. The analysis of the obstacles is tainted by the injection of moral characterizations like "injustice" throughout. The stories of the struggles and successes are viewed as a "distraction." (A distraction? To me, they are the real story, the meaningful and important story.)

Baradaran presents vivid, detailed accounts of examples of Blacks' thrift, initiative, entrepreneurship and resilience. ("Between 1867 and 1917, 4,000 black-owned businesses grew to 50,000. By 1930, the number of black businesses had grown to 70,000." *Id.*, p.51.) These accounts would make a powerful and constructive book.

But, her stories are interspersed with what can most succinctly be called whining. Nothing is ever right. Always too much or too little:

- Black banks were essential/Black banks ruined Black lives;
- Black banks were too conservative/Black banks took too many risks;
- Black businesses were successful because of Black customers/ Black businesses suffered because their customers were Black;
- Black businesses suffered because they had higher costs/Black consumers paid higher prices;
- Blacks had too little access to mortgage financing/Blacks had too much access to mortgage financing;
- Blacks had too little access to revolving credit (credit cards)/Blacks had too much access to revolving credit;
- Jim Crow laws stifled Black businesses/The end of the Jim Crow laws did not eliminate the disadvantages.

Of course, all of these things are true, because the world is complex and messy. But, Baradaran seems to forget that.

She seems to forget that people make mistakes, that capitalism is risky, that businesses fail, that luck can be bad, that the future is uncertain, that shit happens. She bemoans the mistakes and misfortunes that befell the Black businesses and communities. She seems to think that, in contrast, everything went well and easily for white businesses and communities. She ignores the white failures and setbacks.

"Such was the allure of counterfeit capitalism—it had such a convincing semblance to the real thing that it was able to conceal the fact that blacks were still being consumed by capitalism as opposed to fully participating in capital production." *Id.*, p.35.

She sidesteps the implications of the fact that many of the problems were the result of nationwide economic disruptions that affected all businesses. And, of error, mismanagement, unintended consequences, all with respect to government policy, legislation and regulation. Just the normal types of things that regularly go wrong.

"The scheme began to unravel following the Panic of 1873, when railroad investments failed." *Id.*, p. 29.

"The hardships caused by cotton and debt almost erupted into a revolution during the depression of the 1880s and 1890s." *Id.*, p. 34.

"Many of these banks fell, just like their white counterparts, under the stress of the Panic of 1893." *Id.*, p.44.

"The Great Depression brought down both the titans of black finance and the budding shoots of smaller black banks." *Id.*, p. 86.

"By 1970, the country was in a recession. Jobless numbers were so bad by 1971 that the Nixon administration decided to stop reporting them. The new aspiring entrepreneurs in the ghetto suffered most acutely as inflation soared and banks closed the credit pipeline." *Id.*, p. 184.

"Maggie Walker's bank endured the Great Depression and two world wars, but it could not survive the 2008 financial crisis." *Id.*, p. 44.

"The financial crisis of 2008 disproportionately affected segregated black communities and turned the persistent racial wealth gap into a chasm. ...The financial crisis wiped out 53 percent of total black wealth." *Id.*, p.249.

Also, the Panics of 1890 and 1907.

Baradaran then concludes each example with accusations about the motives of other groups and of conspiracies underlying the outcomes.

"Support for black banking and black capitalism have been consistent **policy band-aid** solutions, **a decoy response** to the fundamental challenge of overcoming America's legacy of slavery." *Id.*, p.4 (emphasis added).

"The idea of community self-help, valuable as it was when there was no other choice, has been **deployed cynically** at several pivotal historical moments **to thwart** other, more direct answers to the racial wealth gap." *Id.*, p. (emphasis added)

"The moment the war ended, **nervous cotton interest**s worked in local, state, and national courthouses and legislatures to restore a cotton-growing system as quickly as possible and as close to slavery as permissible. **Across the globe**, cotton traders and capitalists agreed that blacks needed to grow cotton." *Id.*, p.19 (emphasis added).

"They could not be plantation labor if they had capital, which meant that **they were prevented from accruing capital**. Had they had land, they could not have been so easily conscripted back into cotton labor." *Id.*, p.21 (emphasis added).

"Just as the Reconstruction reformers had failed to break the cotton oligarchy and achieve black equality, so too did the Populists. ...They failed because **the established political parties of the North and South** had already understood that **sowing animosity between poor whites and poor blacks** was the easiest way to maintain the status quo and to reject the costly and disruptive demands of a coalition of the poor." *Id.*, p.35 (emphasis added).

> "Southern planters and northern industrialists **joined forces** in maintaining a racial hierarchy that benefited both by preserving the status quo. ...The U.S. Supreme Court **also fell in line...** ." *Id.*, pp.36, 37 (emphasis added).

> "Hemmed in by the walls of Jim Crow, black communities had to create their own financial institutions, but **the injustice of segregation that created these banks** also made them weak." *Id.*, p.46 (emphasis added).

Perhaps, the most striking such assertion is the claim that somehow the pursuit of civil rights for Blacks after the Civil War represented a reversal or betrayal of the goals of the antislavery movement. Clearly, such a view mischaracterizes the objectives of the Abolitionists and antislavery proponents and distorts the nature of the subsequent efforts by Black leaders. There is no promise of economic equality in the Nation's founding documents. I think that almost everyone of any race in the last quarter of the nineteenth century would have been puzzled by the assertion that the struggles were really about property, not freedom. (Other books I have discussed make similar arguments that it was a mistake, perhaps innocent, to have pursued legal emancipation and civil rights rather than compensation.)

> "Moderate northern Republicans began to pivot away from the fight for racial equality and began to see equal citizenship as an end goal to be attained by blacks gradually over time through increased education, work, and the accumulation of property."
>
> ...
>
> "But even as reformers abandoned land and economic reform, they fought for civil rights for blacks in form if not in function. ...The legal right to participate in democracy could not overcome the legal prohibition against engaging in the free market or the gaping gap in wealth.
>
> ...

"Instead of land, freed slaves got rights that they could not use due to their economic and political status at the bottom rung of society."

Id., pp.21, 22 (emphasis added).

Similarly, Baradaran seems to be claiming that President Nixon's promotion of Black capitalism, affirmative action in employment and government contracting and jobs was a complex and successful ruse, whether intentional or fortuitous.

"An expert in political détente, Nixon used black capitalism to let out just enough steam from the pent-up pressure cooker of rage in the poverty-stricken ghetto to squelch the brewing revolution. ...With this one move, Nixon took the sting out of the black radicals' demand for black power, jettisoned Johnson's antipoverty programs, maintained his opposition to integration, and even won the support of many black leaders. Checkmate."

Id., p.191.

Baradaran also attacks the wars on drugs and crime as part of a scheme to emasculate the Black community. I think that accusation is ridiculous. These efforts, in fact, backfired in that the tougher criminal penalties failed to deter young Black men from drug use and related criminal acts. There is no evidence that that result was foreseen, let alone intended.

> "The weeds that grew ...
> did not need to be fed with racism.
> It [*sic*] used the materials available
> —commerce, credit, money, and segregation—
> to regenerate inequality."

Id., p.7.

Baradaran provides clear descriptions of the economic challenges facing Black businesses. There was a role for Black banks because many Black communities were not being served by the existing banks. The Black banks customer base was dominated by small depositors, and the customers were likely to withdraw deposits frequently. The consequence was that the Black banks had to hold larger reserves than other banks meaning higher costs and less money available for loans.

The Black banks faced difficult decisions with respect to their lending practices. They were pressured to lend locally to Black businesses and individuals, but these loans carried greater than average risks. To the extent that the banks sought more secure investments, the money saved within the Black communities would flow out into the broader economy and its productive use would occur elsewhere. Much of the need within the communities was for the funding of mortgages, but again the mortgages tended to be of greater risk levels because of the volatile nature of housing prices in the segregated neighborhoods. The conflicts between service to the community and profitability.

"However, these banks also faced specific challenges. When they began to offer loans, there was often a dangerous conflict of interest. Successful banking relies on good underwriting, or the ability to choose between a profitable loan and a losing loan or a creditworthy borrower and one who is likely to default. ...they often made loan decisions based on factors having less to do with good underwriting and more to do with community need or pressure... ." *Id.*, p.42.

"Concentrated populations of black wage workers proved to be a bounty for the black banks. But that same concentration also created special vulnerabilities." *Id.*, p.70.

"Although Chelsea Exchange Bank took all of Harlem's deposits, it did not make loans to Harlem. ...The Chelsea bank manager responded that the bank's refusal to extend credit to African Americans was not due to prejudice, but rather to the bank's strictly conservative policies." *Id.*, pp.77, 78.

"Black bank deposits differed from those in white banks—they were smaller and were more frequently withdrawn, which made them more risky. ...In order to minimize the risks presented by their small and fickle deposits, bank managers held more capital, cash reserves, and liquid assets. All of this meant that they could make fewer loans and thus were not able to fully enjoy the benefits of fractional reserve lending." *Id.*, pp.88, 89.

"Home loans were inherently risky, but the key problem for black banks was not the proportion of these loans they held, but their nature. ...Members of the black middle class moving into a neighborhood were seen as harbingers of a neighborhood being swallowed by the ghetto. ...These fears turned into self-fulfilling prophesies, because once a neighborhood 'tipped' and was seen as a 'black neighborhood,' whites fled and the neighborhood declined... . ...Data also revealed what was already obvious to the black middle class: that the first blacks to own a home in a formerly white neighborhood paid a premium to buy the home to break the color barrier. So values rose slightly, and then, as more blacks entered the neighborhood, home values suffered a drastic decline." *Id.*, pp.90, 91.

"The crucial difference, one that would perpetually prove insurmountable, was that black banks' assets, loans on black properties, were not appreciating in value." *Id.*, p.95.

"The irony is that black banks, which were created to control the black dollar, were the very mechanism through which black money flowed out of the community." *Id.*, p.96.

"The decision to favor small community banks over larger bank networks was not racially motivated, but it did negatively affect the prospects for black banking." *Id.*, p.124.

"[T]hey had to make sure that a majority of their shareholders were black. This limited their pool of potential investors and diminished their ability to attract capital." *Id.*, p.244.

In the twenty-first century, the trend in Harlem is reversed and rising prices are the problem.

"Indeed, Harlem is experiencing something of a real estate renaissance, which looks more like a transformation. Instead of a smattering of small-scale businesses, Harlem now has large retail outlets, hotels, and businesses that have followed the wave of more prosperous residents. ...[R]esidents are being priced out of Harlem as Manhattan's booming population begins to overflow uptown."

Id., p.270.

Black businesses selling to Black customers often lacked the scale achieved by white businesses, leading to higher costs and, therefore, higher prices. The higher prices were a source of discontent among Black consumers.

Baradaran blames the reliance on installment purchases for greater costs for Black consumers, asserting that whites benefited economically from the availability of credit cards as an alternative to installment purchases. ("The consumer credit market shifted from the rigid and expensive installment lending model to the flexible and less expensive 'revolving credit' enabled by the credit card. ...This was another instance in which the **New Deal credit reforms created** an abundant and low-cost credit market for whites and **an extractive and inescapable debt trap for blacks.**" *Id.*, p.113, emphasis added.)

I am not convinced. Credit card debt can be very expensive, and credit cards can tend to lead to excessive and ruinous debt. Indeed,

> "Consumer loans also came flooding into the ghetto. Where credit card issuers had been avoiding the zip codes where blacks lived, by the 1980s they joined the mortgage lenders and began looking for them. With the usury cap lifted and the general aversion to risk abated, lenders went looking for higher profits on high-risk borrowers. They found their ideal customers in the credit-and wealth-starved ghetto. And when they did, these revolvers, who paid interest each month, began to subsidize the credit cards of the wealthy. Credit issuers pulled on blacks to borrow so that they could profit from the attendant fees and interest. At the same time, blacks were being pushed to borrow by their low and volatile wages."

Id., p.238.

In addition, the exploitation of captive customers is a widespread problem regardless of race, as evidenced by company towns and company stores or the common practice in human trafficking of using debt as chains to ensnare people.

She offers no solutions to these challenges. She attributes them to segregation. They are apparently the inevitable consequences of segregated communities. They presumably would be removed only by complete integration, by the elimination of Black communities, of Black banks. Such a result could not easily be achieved, even if it were determined to be desirable. It would require rather extreme coercion and disregard of individual choice.

Otherwise, Baradaran suggests that compensation, the reallocation of wealth, would be just and a solution to the perceived problems, but she fails to indicate how it would change things going forward, what would be different apart from a sudden, temporary reduction in inequality of wealth. How, if at all, would the dynamics of the country change? What, if any, structural changes would occur? We are left with nothing more than a lengthy complaint about how things are.

> "The wealth gap is where historic injustice
> breeds present suffering." *Id.*, p.1.

What does this statement mean or reveal? "The wealth gap ... breeds present suffering"?

Why? Envy? Manipulation? Who is sowing the seeds of discontent?

It is correct that the government policies implemented with the New Deal and thereafter disproportionately benefited white Americans and failed to benefit Blacks. That fact can be reasonably labeled unfair. However, the repeated assertion that these government benefits or subsidies came "at the expense of" Black Americans is unsupported. (*E.g.*, "Yet this was a manufactured prosperity that left blacks out. It was achieved at their expense." *Id.*, p. 107 (emphasis added).) There is no basis for a claim that these policies made Blacks worse off than they were or otherwise would have been

She sharply criticizes the arguments that welfare dependency was a cause of the deterioration of Black communities. Okay. Let's leave that thesis aside. We do all agree, however, that, first, the programs of President Johnson's Great Society did not solve the problems that Baradaran highlights and, second, the problems of the Black communities have gotten far worse since the 1960s.

So, what is the explanation?

Baradaran argues that the amounts spent were too little, especially since much of the assistance went to poor whites. But, what evidence is there that more public assistance would have altered behavior? I note that a recent study concluded that the discharge of huge medical bills did not lead to greater happiness or, even, improved economic situations. *See* Raymond Kluender, Neale Mahoney, Francis Wong and Wesley Yin, "The Effects of Medical Debt Relief: Evidence from Two Randomized Experiments," *NBER*, April 2024 ("we find no impact of debt relief on credit access, utilization, and financial distress on average ... we find no effect of medical debt relief on mental health on average, with detrimental effects for some groups in pre-registered heterogeneity analysis").

The fundamental flaw and source of misdirection in the "wealth gap" analysis is its underlying conceptualization of the issue as a competition or race. Of course, anyone with a "headstart" will have an advantage in a race, but why is the essence of the matter how one stacks up against another? That seems to place envy as the central fact of life. I suggest that the fair opportunity to improve one's situation or circumstances is the key to satisfaction, that the appropriate comparison is not to others, but to one's past, one's heritage.

I am not asserting that under that standard, all is well; only that the problems and solutions should be assessed within that framework.

CHAPTER 2

Promise Not Realized

I.

"[T]he phenomena that we call life,
consciousness, and intelligence will be shown
to have deep cosmic significance."

...

"The emergence of cognition, and
even intelligence, was just as inevitable
as the emergence of life.

...

"Cosmic teleology is a worldview
that recognizes the goal-directed nature of our universe,
a dynamical system that is becoming increasingly
complex and sentient as time moves forward... ."

Seyed B. Azarian,
The Romance of Reality:
How the Universe Organizes Itself to Create
Life, Consciousness, and Cosmic Complexity
(2022), pp.3, 73, 255 (emphasis added).

"In our quest to understand cosmic evolution, we will arrive at a 'theory of everything' .... This ambitious theory attempts to solve the greatest remaining mysteries of science. The infamous 'hard problem of consciousness,' the puzzle of free will, and the mystery of increasing cosmic complexity in an increasingly entropic universe all begin to unravel as the unifying theory dissolves the paradoxes created by the unjustified assumptions of the reductionist worldview and exposes the language traps that have prevented us from making intellectual progress for so long. ...[T]he unifying theory of reality bridges the gap between the quantum and cosmological with principles from evolutionary biology. ...[A] new scientific and spiritual worldview—called poetic meta-naturalism... .

...

"Poetic meta-naturalism ... argues that **nature has an intrinsic purpose—to wake up and experience the fruits of its own creation.**"

Azarian, pp.6-7, 156 (emphasis added)..

Really? Let's take a look.

The book is full of repetition. There are lengthy, almost poetic sections on important, but noncontraversial, propositions. I felt like I was just wandering. So, I have tried to extract and organize the key points, then analyze the thesis.

Azarian writes:

"Energy flowing through chemical networks forces intricate patterns of biological design into existence... . ...This law has been formalized to some degree, albeit abstractly, in England's work on dissipative adaptation, and also in Bejan's own work, which applies the constructal law to all kinds of systems—chemical, biological, social, economic, even technological."

Azarian, p.138.

I previously wrote about some theories and research addressing the apparent self-organizing tendencies of inanimate matter. (Perhaps, it is more accurate to say the tendency of certain inanimate matter to become organized, *i.e.*, for certain structures to appear.) I discussed in some detail Adrian Bejan's "constructal law" and Jeremy England's "dissipative adaptation." *Important Things We Don't Know About Nearly Everything*, pp.569-71, 543-4, 573-4.

The question is not whether it happens, but why? What mechanism or process is at work? Azarian provides a plausible partial answer. In doing so, he undertakes a rather extended (and interesting) discussion of entropy and the Second Law of Thermodynamics. The point, however, can be more simply made: "Nature ...abhors a gradient" (Azarian, p.21) or, as I prefer, a differential. An existing difference in temperature, pressure, concentration, electrical charge, energy or entropy will naturally tend to disappear, to equalize.

"A gradient is the difference between two interacting systems that creates instability, whether it be a difference in temperature, pressure, chemical concentration, or electrical charge. If such a difference exists, there will be spontaneous flow from one system to the other until that difference, or the gradient, is eliminated, and a stable and inert state of equilibrium is achieved. This happens automatically because nature is simply intolerant of gradients."

Azarian, pp.21-22.

A differential may be stable if a barrier or obstacle separates the two levels, but, if a breach occurs (a hole in the dyke), the differential will disappear as the "matter" from one region "flows" into the other. Azarian argues that such a relationship exists with respect to "free energy" (energy available to do work, like energy flowing from the sun). It will follow pathways to dissipation, generally as heat. If a change in structure occurs by chance that enables the more rapid dissipation of free energy, that new structure will be "favored," that is, will be more stable, more lasting, than the prior structures or arrangements. Thus, in circumstances of disequalibrium, a kind of natural selection will result in disturbances, by trial and error, leading to arrangements that more efficiently dissipate free energy. Those arrangements appear organized.

"How a complex system suddenly transitions into a more organized state is not entirely understood, but it can only occur when the system's components are collectively interacting in such a way that the activity of its parts becomes increasingly coordinated and statistically correlated. ...When the collective effects of these mutually reinforcing interactions reach a critical threshold, in a manner that is purely mechanical but also quite mystical in appearance, global patterns of synchronized activity suddenly emerge, and the system gains some new property or function, appropriately called an emergent property."

Id., p.53.

"Through trial and error, the emergent system inevitably finds arrangements that are better at extracting energy from a fluctuating, statistically noisy stream of energy. Because states that absorb energy are stable, they are selected, and because they create entropy, they are harder to reverse." *Id.*, p.104.

Azarian argues that the relentless pressure to dissipate free energy can cause a process of or like metabolism in a more complex structure, leading to life, since living things are efficient converters of free energy into heat.

"With no life-forms to graze on that energy, untapped gradients created a planetary-scale energy imbalance that caused global thermodynamic instability. As a result of this tension, autocatalytic chemical sets resembling primitive metabolism spontaneously emerged to unlock and dissipate free energy excesses at locations where stress was greatest."

Id., p.50.

Thereafter, "because collective molecular arrangements that can extract accessible energy tend to be more complex, progress toward increasingly sophisticated dissipative structures is not improbable—in far-from-equilibrium conditions it may be unavoidable."

Id., p.54.

So, "A biosphere will tend to produce an increasingly intelligent species, but the route to general intelligence likely follows a different evolutionary path on each life-producing planet. ...We should expect life to readily emerge on planets with geochemical conditions that are sufficiently similar to those on Earth around 3.8 billion years ago."

Id., p.55.

I have discussed the claim of the spontaneous emergence of metabolism in a prior chapter, so let's just assume now that it could have happened. There are then two serious issues concerning what could have happened next.

First, how does the metabolizing structure reproduce? Absent reproduction, this structure, no matter how magnificent, will simply enjoy its individual grandeur in impotent solitude. Second, although Azarian eloquently rhapsodizes about the incredible power of random variation over very long periods of time to explore all avenues for improvement, such exploration must always start from somewhere. And, the then available improvements, given the starting position, may simply be limited. Similarly, some or all of the initial improvements will lead to dead ends. The possibilities may be limitless, it may just not be possible to get there from here.

Azarian's thesis encounters serious tension between two relatively certain facts:

1. "Life appears to have emerged on Earth just about as soon as conditions allowed, which would be a massive coincidence if its emergence was in fact improbable and a product of pure chance." *Id.*, p.15.

2.　"[A]biogenesis doesn't appear to have ever been repeated" (*id.*, p.56); it has occurred only once on Earth.

Azarian asserts that the answer probably is that the first life that arose on Earth spread so rapidly and extensively that the available energy was co-opted foreclosing opportunities for other life to emerge. He is confident that if that first life had suffered extinction, new life would have appeared to fill the space. As support for the hypothesis that life—indeed, intelligent life—is inevitable, this explanation seems to me to be somewhat farfetched and clearly inadequate.

The other strand of Azarian's "theory of everything" is based upon the concept of information (another recently trendy topic). He uses it to address the question "How exactly did molecules acquire agency, control, and purpose? Precisely what process instilled a physical system with goals and the capacity to pursue them?" *Id.*, p.58.

The focus on information has been used as an argument supporting design.

"The relatively recent science of information has given rise to the new formulation of many of the arguments we have been discussing, on issues from biology to physics. *See* Stephen C. Meyer, *Signature in the Cell: DNA and the Evidence for Intelligent Design* (2009); Charles Seife, *Decoding the Universe*, p.385. ...The key to life, as we understand it, is the reproducible genetic code contained in RNA and DNA. So, the need for a designer in this context arises not from the complex or sophisticated ('designed') nature of organs or organisms, but from the appearance of the coded genetic information that enables life. It is 'the mystery of the origin of the information needed to build the first living organism.' Meyer, *Signature in the Cell*, p.14."

...

"Meyer asserts that: 'Intelligence is the only known cause of complex functionally integrated information-processing systems.' *Id.*, p.346."

Important Things We Don't Know, pp.525, 528.

Azarian presents a twist on that argument by finding the design in the supposed purposefulness or direction in the cosmos, as discussed above.

His argument:

1. "[I]t is the capacity to acquire, store, process, and transmit information that separates life from nonlife." *Id.*, p.62.

Well, okay. Not exactly intuitively obvious, but... .

2. Then, "[i]f uncertainty is mathematically equivalent to disorder, and information is a reduction in uncertainty, then information acquisition must be associated with a reduction of disorder." *Id.*, p.66. And, "[k]nowledge is the information we acquire that reduces our uncertainty or ignorance about the world." *Id.*, p. 84.

Okay.

3. Knowledge or information is embedded in or captured by physical structures, including "...DNA, life's original memory system. ...[G]enetic memory accumulates in an evolving population of organisms over many generations, as a result of replication with mutation and natural selection... ." *Id.*, p.92.

So, "[h]ow did biological information, computation, and predictive ability emerge through the thermodynamic processes we've identified as the mechanisms underlying abiogenesis?" *Id.*, p.73.

Azarian reintroduces to the model he previously used of self-correcting, trial and error processes. A version of natural selection goes to work on knowledge (or, more precisely, the physical structures that embody knowledge), leading to wonderous results. "Knowledge ... allows physical systems to be able to experience the world and to generate patterns of activity that have meaning and feeling, thereby transforming nonliving parts of the universe into pieces with purpose." *Id.*, p.155.

[A] self-correcting system grows more robust and computationally powerful because it is always solving survival problems and storing the solutions in memory." *Id.*, p.115

"As the brain encodes adaptive information ..., our mental model of the world, the representation of reality that defines the mind, gets built up and updated continuously... ." *Id.*, p.90.

"This interpretation of the evolutionary process stresses that adaptive systems store a simplified representation or model of the world they inhabit. As evolution and adaptive learning proceed, life is effectively performing statistical inference and updating its model's 'beliefs about the world" *Id.*, p.118

"Essentially, mutation is an inventor and natural selection is a pruner. The genetic and neural information that is left over after natural selection culls the generated biodiversity reflects knowledge of the environment that enables the ordered system to survive and thrive." *Id.*, pp.130-131.

"As external conditions change over time, new adaptive solutions are discovered and written into genetic memory, such that new knowledge is continuously being generated, along with new modes of behavior." *Id.*, p.131.

Where to start?

Perhaps, with some nits. It is troubling to describe the evolution of a bacteria as the acquisition of knowledge. It is even more problematic to characterize the adaptive mutations as being ever-improving "predictors".

"As a species adapts to a niche over many generations, the design and behavior of the prototypical organism becomes more statistically correlated with its environment, and therefore it **becomes a better predictor** of that environment." *Id.*, p.132 (emphasis added).

While the analogy of an increasingly accurate mental model of the environment makes some sense with respect to conscious entities, it is seriously misleading with respect to unconscious life forms. They simply do not compare and select. It happens to them, not by them.

A crucial assumption is that physical changes through trial and error alter the state of the embedded knowledge and that improvements in the knowledge increase the survivability of the host organism. Perhaps. But, I doubt that there is a one-to-one correspondence between physical changes and increased knowledge. Additionally, what could be the source and content of the original model of the environment that is then being improved?

Finally, Azarian's theory does not explain the origin of RNA or DNA. Memory must be available for natural selection to operate. So, from where does it come?

"What makes the idea in this book different, and not just different, but superior... ?" *Id.*, 82. Good question.

As an aside, Azarian asserts that this theory solves the supposed problem of the tautological nature of Darwin's natural selection based on survival of the fitest, in which fitness is defined by the fact of survival. I have previously discussed my view that that apparent tautology is not really problematic (*Important Things*, pp.222-3), but let's look at the proposed solution:

> "The integrated evolutionary synthesis gets rid of the fitness tautology... . From the thermodynamic perspective, fitness pertains to how well an organism can resist entropic decay. In particular, fitness corresponds to the resilience of the embodied energy-extraction program, the dissipative channel, and is not correlated with strength, intelligence, or even complexity."

Id., p.137.

So, we can say "survival of the most resilient embodied energy-extraction program."

Not very catchy. And, hardly less circular. "Resilience" is still not defined independently from the outcome of survival. It does not have its own measurement scale like, for example, "the tallest" or "the strongest."

II.

Helen De Cruz,
Wonderstruck:
How Wonder and Awe Shape the Way We Think
(2024).

I was again misled by a book review. Actually, I remember nothing of the review; I was lured by the title: *Wonderstruck: How Wonder and Awe Shape the Way We Think.*

Awe and wonder. That sounded like a healthy change in my reading. Who would have thought that a book on awe and wonder could be dry, tedious, joyless. The nature of the book revealed itself on the first page. We are presented with the image of a family with young children parading outside to look at the night sky.

> "We all stood in that quiet suburban street in Saint Louis, Missouri, watching for a while, waiting for the blood moon to make a furtive appearance from behind a persistent veil of clouds. Finally, near midnight, we beheld the wine-red disc. My daughter asked, 'So, this is a total lunar eclipse? If it's total, why can I still see the moon?'"

Id., pp.1-2.

I vividly recall my first good look at the night sky. My parents took us to an operating observatory. After seeing the telescopes, we went the observation deck, facing north, i believe. I was stunned. There, too clear, too close, to be real, was The Big Dipper, the North Star, Orion, Cassiopeia's Chair. Unmistakable. It was thrilling. It is unforgettable. And, it was not a feeling of vastness, but of immediacy. Almost a slap in the face.

Years later, camping in the North Woods, one moonless night, I crawled out of the tent to find a world lit by starlight. I could see the whole campsite; there were shadows and the sky was white. Actually, the stars did not blanket the entire sky but the Milky Way was a mottled fabric of stars of different brightnesses. Now this was vastness, but somehow not remote. I did not feel small or insignificant. More like an intrepid adventurer. Confronting the unknown.

I remember my first visit to the Grand Canyon. We went to the North Rim. A long drive through the woods; finally, glimpses of bright colors—oranges, reds, yellows. Then, the large rustic lodge filled my view. In through the lobby, straight ahead, a very large picture window revealed a spectacular panorama of the Canyon. Too vivid and immediate to be real. A photograph? A painting? I rushed outside. There it was. That is what I saw framed by the window. Stunning, overwhelming. I, afraid of heights, stood on a rock outcropping looking almost a mile straight down. No fear, no panic. It wasn't, it couldn't be, real. An illusion? A dream?

Years later, in December, my son, his girlfriend, my daughter and I were making our first ascent of the Pic de Courmettes, the second highest peak in that part of southeastern France where we had a house. The way up was long but scenic. Not too steep. After our lunch break, still a half an hour from the top, surrounded by the light grey stone ruins of shepherds ' shelters and enclosures, I suggested we call it a day. Everyone agreed except my daughter, who defiantly resumed the climb. We followed reluctantly. Huffing and puffing, we finally cleared the summit. There, in the distance, before us spread the snow-covered Italian Alps. We could see forever. We had suddenly emerged into a completely different world. You could feel, smell, taste the change. Absolutely breathtaking.

As to each of these experiences, was my response awe or wonder!? Do we really care?

We are told that awe is "the emotion we sense when we perceive or conceptualize vastness, combined with a need for cognitive accommodation," while wonder is "the emotion that arises from a glimpse at the unknown terrain which lies just beyond the fringes of our current understanding." *Id.*, p.4.

Right.

The book informs of many facts about awe and wonder that we probably did not really want to know. Like, that the ancient world did not distinguish between the two; that Rene Descartes considered wonder a neutral reaction while Adam Smith considered it a negative one, yet Descartes believed that with increased knowledge wonder would (or should) disappear while Smith believed that we would always wonder; that social scientists have spent much more time analyzing awe than they have wonder; that social scientists disagree "on the extent to which a lack of understanding contributes to its aesthetic appeal"; that "there is a small body of empirical and conceptual work that indicates that awe and wonder are distinct emotions"; that "awe and wonder are emotions that we harness by means of cultural practices, that we nurture deliberately, and that are part of a positive feedback loop"; and that "religion can be a cognitive technology that helps us to harness a sense of awe and wonder." *See, e.g., id.*, pp.35, 44, 45, 65, 69, 110.

And, much, much more.

'Descartes defines wonder as follows: Wonder is a sudden surprise of the soul which brings it to consider with attention the objects that seem to it unusual and extraordinary."

"This sense of wonder is, for Smith, a negative emotion: it feels unpleasant to wonder."

"Through the practice of religious habits, we open up new possibilities to experience awe and wonder at things that we've long grown used to. Religious practices can be apt to help us keep bad awe and wonder at bay, while also cultivating awe and wonder that are useful and regulative for us."

Id., pp.34, 40, 110.

Finally,

"Like other emotions, awe and wonder help us to be more effective in our dealings with our environment." *Id.*, p.47. "I think our best guess is that neither awe nor wonder are basic emotions; but that doesn't mean they are not evolutionarily significant." *Id.*, p.70.

Perhaps most frustrating to me is the inadequacies of her discussion of awe and wonder as adaptive developments of *homo sapiens*. She observes, and discusses several analyses of, the possible evolutionary roles of awe and wonder. Pretty weak stuff. As I have previously written, I consider these capacities to be hallmarks of the uniqueness of human consciousness. *Important Things We Don't Know*, pp.584-96. That is the matter of most interest and of most consequence—the role of awe and wonder in the emergence of human consciousness. (The observation that other animals seem to display curiosity does not suffice. *See* De Cruz, p.5.)

CHAPTER 3

Questions Unanswered

MYSTERIES OF THE CELL

I.

Multi-cell Organisms

"A life within a life.
An independent living being ...
that forms a part of the whole."

...

"The life of an organism reposes
in the life of a cell."

Siddhartha Mukherjee
The Song of the Cell:
An Exploration of Medicine and the New Human
(2022), pp.xiv, 12.

The cell is the basis of life—of all life, at least as we know it. Every living thing is composed of cells. It is possible that there might be life somewhere in the Universe that exists without cells, but it is hard to imagine what it could be like.

"[S]mall, containing between one or two and up to about twenty carbon atoms, but most of them have fewer than ten carbons. Think of these as carbon 'skeletons', in which the carbon is bound to itself plus hydrogen and oxygen atoms.... . These are the building blocks that make up cells, little more than a few hundred types of molecule in total."

Nick Lane, *Transformer: The Deep Chemistry of Life and Death* (2022), p. 9.

All cells derive from other cells, either through cell division ("mitosis"), in which a cell "bulks up" then divides into two identical cells, or through reproduction ("meiosis"), where two cells combine and create a new cell with genetic content coming half from each parent.

"In mitosis, ... [y]ou start, say, with forty-six (the number of chromosomes in human cells); the chromosomes duplicate (ninety-two), and then each daughter cell gets half: back to forty-six."

...

"The genesis of sperm and eggs ... require first halving the number of chromosomes, twenty-three each, and then restoring them back to forty-six upon fertilization."

Mukherjee, pp.99, 100.

It is possible that the cell emerged independently on several occasions; however, if that happened, one would expect detectable structural differences to exist. In cells today, such differences have not been found, indicating that all cells existing today in animals, plants or as single-celled organisms have derived from a single original cell.

Incredible.

"All complex life on earth shares a common ancestor, a cell that arose from simple bacterial progenitors on just one occasion in 4 billion years. ...We now know that eukaryotes all share a common ancestor... . Let me reiterate this point, as it is crucial. All plants, animals, algae, fungi and protists share a common ancestor—the eukaryotes are monophyletic. ...[A] population of morphologically complex eukaryotic cells arose on a single occasion—and all plants, animals, algae and fungi evolved from this founder population. Any common ancestor is by definition a singular entity—not a single cell, but a single population of essentially identical cells."

Nick Lane, *Vital Question: Energy, Evolution, and the Origins of Complex Life* (2015), pp.1, 39, 40.

"Take a yeast cell or some species of single-celled algae. These single cells, or modern cells, as biologist Nick Lane calls them, possess virtually all the features of the cells of vastly more complex organisms, including humans."

Mukherjee, pp. 130-131.

The miracle of the cell includes the fact that cells can and do get together to form multicellular organisms.

"Why did we ever leave the single-celled world? Why did 'we' become 'we'—that is, multicellular organisms?" Mukherjee, p.130.

I use "get together" very loosely. In fact, cells of a particular type can clump together forming larger entities. Examples are so-called Snowflake yeast and algae. Now, these clumps consist of multiple identical cells, but at a certain point, the aggregate can start acting as an entity separate from the individual cells, doing things that cannot be done by the cells individually. We can imagine some survival benefits in being an aggregate, for example:

> "that multicellularity evolved to support larger sizes and rapid movement, thereby enabling the organism to escape predation ... or to make faster, coordinated movements toward weak gradients of food. Evolution raced toward collective existence because 'organisms' could race away from being eaten—or, equally, race toward eating."

Id., p.134.

"Leaflike 'organisms' with radiating structures resembling small veins (veinules) and containing multiple cells, appeared about 570 million years ago and flourished on ocean floors. Sponges agglomerated out of individual cells. Colonies of microorganisms organized themselves into novel 'beings,' heralding a new kind of existence."

Id., p. 131.

Curiously, we also find that some specialization can begin to appear among cells within the aggregation.

"In one of the most intriguing attempts, carried out at the University of Minnesota in 2014, a group of researchers led by Michael Travisano and

William Ratcliff made a multicellular being evolve from a unicellular organism." *Id.*, p.132.

Growing yeast cells in flasks (actually, letting them multiply), they observed that some mother /daughter cells stuck together after the cell division. The researchers collected the cell clumps and then grew those in flasks. They continued to repeat the process over and over. The first result was the appearance of really large aggregates. The next result was that a certain size, the aggregates would split in two. The two halves would keep growing. The third result was the aggregates came to exhibit a phenomenon in which a line of cells across the middle of the aggregate would die, facilitating the division of the aggregate.

Note that this experiment is not evolution by natural selection. It is more like selective breeding (without a male and female).

One could imagine that some random mutations in a few cells may have proven beneficial to the survival of the aggregate and became survivors, but that is not what seems to be happening. Instead, the changes that enable specialization appear to be potentials lying dormant in the individual identical cells.

If the result of evolution, then there must have been either (i) an adaptive mutation that benefited the individual cell and incidentally turned out to benefit the aggregate or (ii) at some prior time, the aggregates existed and a mutation in cell benefited the aggregate, leading to more successful aggregates which at some later point dispersed into individual cells carrying the mutation. How, then, did that mutated cell fair among its unmutated relatives? Rather complicated and speculative.

Unfortunately, I do not think that this line gets us to true multicell organisms. This example would be more relevant if reproduction occurred through the separation from the aggregate of a single cell that then commenced to "grow" into a new aggregate.

There is no doubt but that multi-cell organisms enjoy important benefits beyond size. Specialization of cells and division of labor would likely increase efficiency in biology, just as they do in human enterprises. There may even be opportunities for economies of scale. But, what's in it for the individual cell? Adaptive changes may promote the reproduction of the multicellular organism, but will the individual cell benefit? Certainly, single-celled life has not disappeared.

Now jump ahead to today's most sophisticated multicellular organisms—mammals. The complex organism arises from a single fertilized cell, which begins to divide. The descendant cells, all identical at creation, begin to specialize, forming a heart, kidneys, a liver, blood, capillaries, skin and a brain. The list goes on. How did the potential for all these diverse functions and designs get incorporated into that single fertilized egg?

So, the question of how multicellular organisms arose becomes more significant.

> "But perhaps the most astonishing feature of multi-
> cellularity is that it evolved independently, and in multiple
> different species, not just once, but many, many times.
> ...Collective existence—above isolation—was so selectively
> advantageous that the forces of natural selection gravitated
> repeatedly toward the collective."

Id., p.131.

Mukherjee asserts: "[T]he evolution of multicellularity was not an accident, but purposeful and directional." *Id.*, p.135. Really? What is the "purpose" and from where did it come? Who or what provided the "direction"? And, while we are at it, what is the direction?

Well, the sentence has a nice ring to it, even if it makes no sense.

II.

The Modern Cell

"Few things are as inscrutable as a cell."

Nick Lane
Transformer:
The Deep Chemistry of Life and Death
(2022), p.3.

"The origin of the modern cell
is an evolutionary mystery.
It seems to have left only the scarcest
of fingerprints of its ancestry or lineage,
with no trace of a second or third cousin,
no close-enough peers that are still living,
no intermediary forms."

Siddhartha Mukherjee
The Song of the Cell,
(2022), p. 72.

Life appeared on Earth perhaps as long as 4 billion years ago, when Earth was less than a billion years old. It consisted of single-celled organisms without a nucleus.

And, from where could that first cell have come? We consider that question in the next section.

Over the next billion years, what are now called prokaryotes evolved.

"The first cells—the simplest, most primitive of our ancestors—arose on Earth some 3.5 to 4 billion years ago, about 700 million years after the birth of the Earth.

...

"Evolution would select more and more complex features of the cell, eventually replacing RNA with DNA as the information carrier. ...Bacteria evolved out of that simple progenitor about 3 billion years ago... .

Mukherjee, p. 70.

"Life arose around half a billion years after the earth's formation, perhaps 4 billion years ago, but then got stuck at the bacterial level of complexity for more than 2 billion years, half the age of our planet. Indeed, bacteria have remained simple in their morphology (but not their biochemistry) throughout 4 billion years."

Nick Lane, *Vital Question* (2015), p.1.

There were two varieties—bacteria and (what we now call) archaea. They are superficially identical, but there are structural differences suggesting independent origination. And, the archaea are more complex. These life forms persisted and thrived alone for another billion years and continue today along side of the newer eukaryotes.

"This new group might have lacked the complexity of eukaryotes, but the genes and proteins that they did have were shockingly different from those of bacteria. This second group of simple cells became known as the archaea, on the hunch that they're even older than the bacteria, which is probably not true; modern views have it that they are equally old. But at the arcane level of their genes and biochemistry, the gulf between bacteria and archaea is as great as that between bacteria and eukaryotes (us). ...[A]rchaea have a few sophisticated molecular machines resembling those of eukaryotes, if with fewer parts – the seeds of eukaryotic complexity."

Id., pp.8, 9.

Then, about 2 billion years ago, a new type of organism appeared, called eukaryotes, comprised of cells with nuclei. They were still presumably quite simple structures.

All three life forms coexisted and thrived.

To the surprise of many biologists, genetic analyses have apparently established with relative certainty that the eukaryotes were created by the combination of an archaeon cell and a bacterial cell (a process called endosymbiosis), with the bacterial cell shedding its no longer needed genetic material to become what we call mitochondria. Subsequently, a second endosymbiosis occurred between this eukaryotes and a bacteria containing chloroplasts. This organism became capable of photosynthesis, converting the energy in sunlight into energy that could power life. Any energy constraints on life were thereby eliminated.

"Over the last few years, comparisons of large numbers of genes in more representative samples of species have come to the unequivocal conclusion that the host cell was in fact an archaeon—a cell from the domain Archaea.

All archaea are prokaryotes. By definition, they don't have a nucleus or sex or any of the other traits of complex life.... In terms of its morphological complexity, the host cell must have had next to nothing. Then, somehow, it acquired the bacteria that went on to become mitochondria. Only then did it evolve all those complex traits."

...

"This radical proposition—complex life arose from a singular endosymbiosis between an archaeon host cell and the bacteria that became mitochondria—was predicted by the brilliantly intuitive and free-thinking evolutionary biologist Bill Martin, in 1998.... .

...

"Chloroplasts are found only in algae and plants, hence were most likely acquired in an ancestor of those groups alone. That puts them as a relatively late acquisition. Mitochondria, in contrast, are found in all eukaryotes ... and so must have been an earlier acquisition.

...

"[S]omehow, it acquired the bacteria that went on to become mitochondria. Only then did it evolve all those complex traits."

Id., p.10.

Endosymbiosis, the successful combination of two organisms into one, is an extremely rare, arguably a"freak," occurrence. *Id.*, p.234. It may have happened only twice in 4 billion years among many, many billions of organisms. (Curiously, it has been reported in April 2024 that researchers have observed in a lab a third occurrence of Endosymbiosis, with an algae cell incorporating a bacterial cell, perhaps enabling the conversion of nitrogen in its metabolism. Of course, it is far too soon to conclude that it will be successful.)

"Endosymbiosis where the host life form becomes fundamental to another organism's function has only happened three known times. ...The first event was roughly 2.2 billion years ago ... when a single-celled organism called archaea swallowed up a bacterium that eventually became the mitochondria. ...Th[e] second event occurred when more advanced cells absorbed cyanobacteria. Cyanobacteria can harvest energy from sunlight and they eventually become organelles called chloroplasts... .

...

"[Researchers claim to have] observed primary endosymbiosis–two lifeforms merging into one organism. This incredibly rare event occurred between a type of abundant marine algae and a bacterium was observed in a lab setting."

...

"With this latest endosymbiosis event, it's possible that the algae is converting nitrogen from the atmosphere into ammonia that it can use for other cellular processes ... [with] the help of a bacterium. "

Laura Baisas , "For the first time in one billion years, two lifeforms truly merged into one organism," *Popular Science,* April 18, 2024.

Thereafter, a new type of eukaryotes appeared, with all the features of a modern cell. How?

Presumably, the new eurokrotes began to evolve. The host archaea had a more complex structure than did bacteria. The membrane of the bacteria may have formed the membrane of a new feature, the nucleus. That membrane could have protected the DNA of the host archaea from contamination by other components of the bacteria. The incorporated bacteria presumably gradually shed genes that were no longer useful, thereby conserving energy. The process remains a mystery because no intermediary organisms have survived. Nick Lane theorizes that the intermediaries were not sufficiently stable to last. So, we jump straight to a fully developed modern cell. (The few organisms that look like intermediaries have apparently been shown to be later in time, being modern cells that subsequently lost features not beneficial in the niches they came to occupy.)

"About 2 billion years ago (once again the exact date is a matter of debate), evolution took a strange and inexplicable turn. That is when a cell that is the common ancestor of human cells, plant cells, fungi cells, animal cells, and amoebal cells appeared on Earth." Mukherjee, p. 71.

"[M]itochondria and chloroplasts were indeed derived from bacteria by endosymbiosis, but that the other parts of complex cells probably evolved by conventional means. The question is: when, exactly? " Lane, *Vital Question*, pp.9-10.

It appears that, in the end, there was an organism that was to be the common ancestor of all eurokrotes existing today. That last common ancestor had essentially all of the characteristics of a modern cell and, presumably, then evolved by natural selection into all of the diverse forms of complex life the Earth has known.

> "We know that the common ancestor had a nucleus, where it stored its DNA. The nucleus has a great deal of complex structure that is again conserved right across eukaryotes. It is enclosed by a double membrane, or rather a series of flattened sacs that look like a double membrane but are in fact continuous with other cellular membranes. The nuclear membrane is studded with elaborate protein pores and lined by an elastic matrix; and within the nucleus, other structures such as the nucleolus are again conserved across all eukaryotes."

Lane, *Vital Question*, p.40.

"All these genomes lead back to the last common ancestor of eukaryotes, which had more or less everything. But where did all these parts come from? The eukaryotic common ancestor might as well have jumped, fully formed, like Athena from the head of Zeus. ...How and why did the nucleus evolve? What about sex? Why do virtually all eukaryotes have two sexes? Where did the extravagant internal membranes come from? How did the cytoskeleton become so dynamic and flexible? Why does sexual cell division ('meiosis') halve chromosome numbers by first doubling them up? Why do we age, get cancer, and die? For all its ingenuity, phylogenetics can tell us little about these central questions in biology."

Id., p.43.

Biochemists ponder the questions of what are the constraints that have kept the bacteria and archaea from becoming bigger and more complex for billions of years and what is different about eurokrotes? The answers would appear to lie in the role of mitochondria. But, I stop here. (Lane does not.)

The incredible story seems to be that the cell appears to have arisen only once on Earth; the pathway to complex cells also appears to have arisen only once and evolution of that cell resulted, not in a tree of life, but in a single Common Ancestor. Just freak occurrences? One after another.

III.

Metabolism

"And yet underneath it all,
we are barely any closer to understanding
what breathes life into these flicks of matter."

...

"Metabolism is what keeps us alive
– it is what being alive is –
the sum of the continuous transformations
of small molecules on a timescale of nanoseconds... ."

Nick Lane
Transformer
(2022), pp.3, 8.

As I previously described in my first book, there is debate about which part of the cell came first. *Important Things We Don't Know About Nearly Everything,* p.540. One important, but still unresolved, issue is whether metabolism (the flow of energy) arose before, and led to the creation of, genetic information or genetic information enabled the emergence of metabolism. The answer to that question would have significance to theories of the appearance of life.

"These three components (a membrane, an RNA information carrier, and a duplicator) might have defined the first cell. If a self-replicating RNA system were bound by a spherical membrane, it would make more RNA copies within the confines of the sphere and grow in size by enlarging the membrane." Mukherjee, *The Song of the Cell*, p.70.

"First, life arose very early ... on a water world not unlike our own. Second, by 3.5 to 3.2 billion years ago, bacteria had already invented most forms of metabolism, including multiple forms of respiration and photosynthesis. For a billion years the world was a cauldron of bacteria, displaying an inventiveness of biochemistry that we can only wonder at." Nick Lane, *Vital Question*, p.29.

Nick Lane is decidedly in the priority of metabolism camp. (I do not attempt to summarize his arguments, but I do note that his discussion is exhaustive and remarkably even-handed.)

"We need the essential elements for the chemical reactions to be readily available. Since these reactions are not spontaneous, the question is what starts the cycles running?" Lane, *Transformer*, p.153. Lane says it is the environment. "Metabolism is driven forwards not by itself, but by the environment—ultimately, by the pressure of hydrogen." *Id.*

"The glorious hypothesis that cells are animated by the continuous directed flow of simple materials and energy turned out to be true for all life." ..."[T]he biochemical pathways that produce the basic building blocks of life are indeed conserved across practically all cells." ..."[P]erhaps the most extraordinary fact is that all cells share the same basic road plan, at least for the city centre itself." *Id.* p. 17.

"We now know that respiration takes place in the mitochondria, the so-called 'powerhouses' of the cell... ." *Id.*, p.32.

Adenosine triphosphate ("ATP") is the energy storage and delivery system used in the cells of all known living organisms, an essential feature of life. It works like a rechargeable battery, discharging or releasing energy as needed by the cell and then recharging from the available energy source to be able to deliver that energy to the cell again. Cycling continuously.

Three phosphate groups are linked to one another by two high-energy bonds. ATP becomes adenosine diphosphate ("ADP") when one of the three phosphate molecules breaks free. That releases energy. (Similarly, energy is released when a phosphate is removed from ADP to form adenosine monophosphate ("AMP").) ADP (and AMP) becomes ATP when one (or two) phosphate molecules are added back. When ADP becomes ATP, what was previously a low-energy molecule becomes a high-energy molecule. ADP is constantly recycled back into ATP.

What is the source from which the energy to convert ADP (or AMP) back into ATP, to enable the reattachment of the phosphates? For plants, it is the Sun; for animals, it is the food they eat.

"[O]xygenic photosynthesis. Silently humming in trees and algae and cyanobacteria, all use virtually the same machinery to fix CO_2 and generate ATP. Oxygen is the waste product.... . [T]hat oxygen does not come from CO_2 —it comes from water, which is split apart to extract the hydrogen—2H."

...

"Literally a transducer, chlorophyll absorbs a photon of light, red light, which excites an electron. The excited electron, zapped away from its former owner, is swiftly spirited off down an electron-transport chain embedded in the membrane."

...

"[T]he power of the sun sets electrons flowing from water ... to synthesise ATP in the first photosystem, and then reduce ferredoxin in the second. By transferring electrons from water right through the two photosystems linked in series ... oxygenic photosynthesis frees life from its hydrothermal roots."

Id., pp.173-174, 174, 175.

But, how does it happen?

Lane focuses on cycles, where the reactions return the chemicals to the starting conditions, ready to repeat the same reactions again. There are two different types of phenomena involved. One is called the "Krebs cycle," in which catalysts in a series of steps convert the inputted molecule into different compounds, releasing protons and electrons (essentially, splitting hydrogen atoms). The process continues in a circle. When the starting point is reached, the missing photons and electrons are replaced from another inputted source. A continuous cycle is created.

"The process by which glucose is oxidised goes like this. First, the C6 glucose [a sugar with 6 carbons] is split into two molecules of the C3 pyruvate, each of which is broken down to acetyl CoA. These are then fed into the Krebs cycle. One complete spin of the cycle (from pyruvate) generates three molecules of CO_2 and five sets of 2H, equivalent to five molecules of H_2. This hydrogen is then fed to oxygen to generate energy, in the form of ATP, via cellular respiration."

Lane, Transformer, p. 57.

"The Krebs cycle and cellular respiration take place inside the mitochondria ... .[T]hey brought along their bacterial metabolism to the ancestor of complex (eukaryotic) cells two billion years ago. ...The Krebs cycle supplies precursors for the synthesis of amino acids, fats, sugars and more." Id., pp.70, 71, 72.

"If, in the first few steps of a cycle beginning with citrate, two CO_2 molecules and multiple sets of 2H are stripped out, then one full turn of the cycle would need to replenish those same constituents, or it would not be a cycle at all. But the carbon, hydrogen and oxygen that have to be replenished do not need to come in the same molecular form... ." Id., p.53.

The second phenomenon is the formation of a photon differential between the two sides of a membrane which permits the transfer of electrons but not protons. So, one side has electrons seeking a place to attach (an acidic solution) and the other side has photons also seeking a home (a base or alkaline solution). Then numerous tiny ports in the membrane "pump" photons across the membrane. Astonishingly, the result is a significant electrical charge across the membrane, caused by the movement not of electrons, but of photons.

"To burn the 2H derived from the Krebs cycle, a membrane was needed." *Id.*, p.63.

"[]The 2H (derived from the Krebs cycle...) are split into their component protons and electrons. The electrons are transferred to oxygen by way of the respiratory chain of carriers embedded in the membrane itself–an electrical current, insulated by the surrounding lipids. This electrical current powers the extrusion of protons across the membrane." *Id.*, 64.

"The protons accumulate outside, giving a difference in proton concentration (which is to say, pH) between the inside and outside. Critically, because protons are positively charged, their accumulation outside generates an electrical charge across the membrane, analogous to a battery. Finally, the flow of protons back through protein turbines embedded in the membrane powers the synthesis of ATP... . Only then are protons reunited with electrons on oxygen, to form water." *Id.*, 64, 65.

"The energy released by the reaction between 2H (extracted from Krebs cycle intermediates) and oxygen is transduced into an electrical charge on the membrane. This charge is awesome." *Id.*, p.68.

The Krebs cycle can spin in reverse, using 2H and CO^2 to form organic molecules.

"[A] revolutionary series of papers stretching back to 1966 ... showed that in some ancient bacteria the Krebs cycle can spin in reverse–rather than stripping 2H and CO2 from food to generate energy, it uses energy to react 2H and CO2 to form organic molecules." *Id.*, p.73.

"The discovery of non-photosynthetic bacteria in deep-sea hydrothermal vents that fix CO2 by way of the reverse Krebs cycle overhauls that conclusion. These bacteria don't need the sun to make their ATP and ferredoxin–they can do it by ancient chemistry alone." *Id.*, p.110.

And, it did so.

IV.

The Origin of Life

Much speculation and experimentation has been devoted to attempting to demonstrate that a cell could emerge spontaneously under naturally occurring circumstances. Some progress has been achieved with respect to membranes, RNA and amino acids, as I have previously described. *Important Things*, pp.541-2. But, I think it fair to say that the "spark of life" (metabolism) has remained elusive.

"As soon as some form of hereditary material has arisen—whether DNA or something else—then the trajectory of evolution becomes unconstrained by information and unpredictable from first principles. What actually evolves will depend on the exact environment, the contingencies of history, and the ingenuity of selection." Lane, *Vital Question*, p.23.

Biochemist Nick Lane has a theory as to how life first arose on Earth. He presents it carefully and cautiously, surrounded by caveats. His discussion is remarkably objective and even-handed. *Vital Question* (2015).

Science writer and commentator "Bobby" (Seyed B.) Azarian, whole heartedly embraces an older version of that theory and presents a seriously oversimplified account of it as part of, and in support of, a much grander, more ambitious claim (discussed in Chapter 5, below). *The Romance of Reality: How the Universe Organizes Itself to Create Life, Consciousness, and Cosmic Complexity* (2024). Azarian's description of this story of the origin of life is so articulate and clear, despite its errors, that I quote it as the introduction to my discussion here:

> "The abject failure to re-create life in the lab suggested that its emergence could not have been the simple result of a warm pond getting hit by jolts of lightening, or even strong and steady sunlight... ...[A]ttempts to manufacture a cell have ultimately been unsuccessful.
>
> ...
>
> "How the first life-form got its energy was a great mystery until a new piece of the puzzle emerged in 1977, when eco-systems filled with new exotic life-forms were discovered deep in the ocean in conditions previously thought to be too extreme to support biology. ...[B]acteria called reductive autotrophs ... feed on the reservoirs of geothermal and geochemical energy produced by the mixing of hot magma, seawater, and rock minerals ... [and] require neither sunlight nor other organisms to sustain themselves.
>
> ...

"The hot and chemically diverse environment would provide not only the molecular building blocks, such as carbon, hydrogen, oxygen, nitrogen, and phosphorus, required for abiogenesis, but also the high temperatures and pressures needed to organize them into a complex reaction network ... .[T]heir rocky structures contained countless pores that could function as compartments where auto-catalytic sets might form.... . ...[T]he rocks provided mineral compounds and other small molecules that could act as catalysts... ."

Azarian, pp.45, 47, 48, 48-49, 50.

However, Lane's theory is that life originated in "alkaline hydro-thermal vents," not in the better known deep-sea thermal chimneys nicknamed "black smokers" where life was found in 1977.

"The discovery of submarine vents in the late 1970s came as a shock, not because their presence was unsuspected (plumes of warm water had betrayed their presence) but because nobody anticipated the brutal dynamism of 'black smokers', or the overwhelming abundance of life clinging precariously to their sides.

...

"Yet these vents, too, are misleading. They are not really cut off from the sun. The animals that live here rely on symbiotic relationships with bacteria that oxidise the hydrogen sulphide gas emanating from the smokers. ...The stunning eruption of life around these black smoker vents is therefore completely, albeit indirectly, dependent on the sun."

Lane, *Vital Question*, pp.103-4.

The submarine alkaline vent was discovered in 2000.

"[A]lkaline vents have **nothing to do with magma...** . They are **not superheated, but warm**, with temperatures of 60 to 90°C. They are not open chimneys, venting directly into the sea, but riddled with a labyrinth of interconnected micropores. And they are not acidic, but strongly alkaline. ...And the vents persist for millennia... ." *Id.*, pp.109, 110 (emphasis added).

"Alkaline vents are not produced by the interactions of water with magma but by a much gentler process – a chemical reaction between solid rock and water. Rocks derived from the mantle, rich in minerals such as olivine, react with water to become the hydrated mineral serpentinite.

...

"Olivine is rich in ferrous iron and magnesium. The ferrous iron is oxidised by water to the rusty ferric oxide form. **The reaction is exothermic (releasing heat), and generates a large amount of hydrogen gas, dissolved in warm alkaline fluids containing magnesium hydroxides.**"

Id., p.108 (emphasis added).

Lane approaches the issues from his expertise in chemistry. That perspective and knowledge permits quite interesting insights into the phenomena in question. For example, he notes that the production of organic materials (consisting of long chains of carbon atoms) requires the combination of hydrogen and carbon dioxide which would be unlikely in the presence of oxygen because the chemical attraction of oxygen and hydrogen (producing water) is too strong.

"The chances of life starting on an oxygenated planet is arguably close to zero: hydrogen must react with CO2 to form organic molecules, but does so very reluctantly if at all in the presence of oxygen, which reacts with H2 far more avidly than does CO2."

...

"Organic molecules don't usually part with single electrons (they deal almost exclusively with pairs of electrons) hence they do not react easily with oxygen. That's why we don't spontaneously combust, and why oxygen can accumulate in the air to such high levels. But of course organic material will burn if set alight with a spark. ... Respiration is a controlled form of combustion. ...It's sobering to realise that without the quantum rules that govern the predominantly two-electron chemistry of carbon, versus the one-electron behaviour of oxygen, the world that we know and love could not exist."

Lane, *Transformer* (2022), pp.158, 159.

He also explains why carbon is a compelling choice for the building blocks of organisms (the large number of potential connection points for other atoms, including other carbon atoms). So, Lane talks a lot about the behavior of electrons. (Also protons, the relative presence of which determines the pH or acidity of a solution).

This type of analysis leads him to the conclusion that the desirable environment for the emergence of life would be a slightly alkaline solution with plenty of CO^2, a supply of H^2 and a steady flow of free energy. Then, one would need some physical enclosure to allow the concentration of resulting materials and to keep out contaminants. So, "[a]lkaline hydrothermal vents provide **exactly the conditions required for the origin of life**: a high flux of carbon and energy that is physically channelled over inorganic catalysts, and constrained in a way that permits the accumulation of high concentrations of organics." *Id.*, p.110.

The Earth 4 billion years ago was largely covered in water. There was no oxygen present, but there was an abundance of CO^2.

> "In terms of thermodynamics, CO2 will react with hydrogen (H2) to form methane (CH4). ...Four billion years ago, the moderate temperatures and anoxic conditions in alkaline vents should have favoured the reaction of CO2 with H2 to form CH4. ...But—and this is a big but—H2 does not easily react with CO2. There is a kinetic barrier... . ...H2 and CO2 are practically indifferent to each other. To force them to react together requires an input of energy... ."

Id., pp.113-4.

> "[B]acteria growing from H2 and CO2 can only grow when powered by a proton gradient across a membrane. ...The proton concentration—the acidity—is different on opposite sides of the membrane. ...[G]iven this difference in pH, it is quite easy for H2 to reduce CO2 to make formaldehyde. The only question is: how are electrons physically transferred from H2 to CO2? The answer is in the structure. FeS minerals in the thin inorganic dividing walls of microporous vents conduct electrons. ...And so in theory, **the physical structure of alkaline vents should drive the reduction of CO2 by H2, to form organics... .**"

Id., pp.117-8 (emphasis added).

"[T]he physical structure of alkaline vents—natural proton gradients across thin semiconducting walls—will (theoretically) drive the formation of organics. And then concentrate them. ... Add to this the fact that all life on earth uses (still uses!) proton gradients across membranes to drive both carbon and energy metabolism... ."

Id., p.120.

"The combination of high CO_2, mildly acidic oceans, alkaline fluids, and thin, FeS-bearing vent walls is crucial, because it promotes chemistry that would otherwise not happen easily." *Id.,* p.113.

"And we have indeed produced formate, formaldehyde and other simple organics (including ribose and deoxyribose). ...There should be a slow but sustained synthesis of organic molecules." *Id.,* p.119.

Perhaps, metabolism arose in the pores (micro-vents) of an alkaline vent. It sounds plausible. But, that is still not life.

What might have happened next? Lane speculates that in some cases a membrane developed, freeing the metabolizing process from its rock home, enabling it to float away. If that bubble somehow acquired the capacity to reproduce, then it could populate the seas. Now, that involves some serious unexplained events.

So, maybe we have identified a path by which life could have arisen on Earth. Maybe. But, contrary to the extravagant claims by Azarian, I do not think that this theory, even if empirically confirmed, resolves the "fine-tuning" problem (it simply adds additional preconditions, although ones that maybe are less improbable than the others); establishes that life, let alone complex life, was inevitable (especially given that the modern cell appears to have emerged only once in billions of years and that bacteria and archaea have remained largely the same during that time) or, therefore, that life must exist elsewhere in the Universe.

CHAPTER 4

More Questions

I.

CONSCIOUSNESS

"This rejection of the reality of lived experience
constitutes a mind-boggling repudiation
of what is immediately and indubitably given to us.
It is also profoundly antihumanist, depriving
us of those attributes that make us different from machines
—indeed, equating us with machines."

...

"Any -ism that fails to explain the qualitative, felt
aspects of pain, despair, distress, despondency,
suffering, trauma, loss, and melancholy
does not account for the human condition."

Christof Koch
Then *I Am Myself the World:
What Consciousness Is and How to Expand It*
(2024), pp.2, 80.

"But the soul?
How can the soul be an illusion?
How can consciousness be just a
mechanical play of atoms and molecules?
...I may be mistaken about what
I see or feel or think or wish,
but that I see, feel, think, or wish
I cannot be mistaken. ...The world,
myself, all life, all history, and all science
may well be images and thoughts
happening in a dream.
But the dream itself is real.
My consciousness,
whether I am dreaming or awake,
is real. ...There is no explaining consciousness
by atoms and the void."

Giulio Tononi
Phi: A Voyage from the Brain to the Soul
(2012), p.22.

I have written quite a bit, directly and indirectly, about consciousness. *See Important Things We Don't Know*, pp.433-92, 584-600; *Imaginings*, pp.133-77. Yet, there seems always to be more to say. What has already been said just seems inadequate. It is. We simply do not have answers to the fundamental questions.

The paradoxes are striking:

• If mind and body are separate and distinct, as dualism asserts, then how does the mind cause the body to do things, which believers in free will assert it certainly does. By what mechanism can the immaterial affect the material? If there is no free will, then the separate mind is an illusion or is just irrelevant.

- Subjective experience is arguably the only thing we can know is real. Everything else could be a simulation or an illusion. This was the shocking conclusion of Descartes. *"Cogito, ergo sum,* or 'I think, therefore I am,' the most famous deduction in Western thought."* Koch, p.73. (Even if the simulation triggers a feeling, the feeling itself is real, not simulated.) Yet, the subjective feelings of other people are impossible for us to know. Even the consciousness of others can only be assumed, not demonstrated. Thus, the essence of the zombie problem—we must believe that zombies (entities that are indistinguishable from humans but are not conscious) could exist because we cannot prove that someone else is not a zombie. So, consciousness must exist separately from the body.

"[T]he act of perception alone means that the observer is real, even if what he or she is observing is not. ...You can doubt almost everything about existence, but you can't doubt that you exist. Consciousness cannot be denied or explained away." Bobby Azarian, *The Romance of Reality: How the Universe Organizes Itself to Create Life, Consciousness, and Cosmic Complexity* (2024), p.190.

- If consciousness is merely a phenomenon resulting from physical processes (say, through feedback loops in neural networks), then how do we make choices? Do we not have free will, even though we know that we do?

And, so on and on.

Koch writes:"Peering even deeper, with an atomic force microscope, individual macromolecules come into focus. But never pain, pleasure, or ennui." *Id.*, p. 74.

Clever. But, actually, we can see none of the results of neural activity. All that we can ever see are the patterns of the activity. If we discover that a particular pattern is regularly associated with a specific experience, like pain in the lower right leg, we will begin to think that we "see" the feeling when we observe that pattern. In the same manner, if we found the neural signature for *ennui*, we could see the feeling. We do not know whether there are, in fact, distinctive patterns of activity for particular feelings (Koch seems to suggest that the numerous differences among people make it unlikely); but, in all events, we still have not explained the mechanism that gives rise to feelings.

Consciousness includes:

1. Self-awareness, me versus everyone and everything else, everything not me.

"The 'self' that is the observer arises from the self-referential act of self-modeling. By introducing the idea of an internally embedded world model, the unifying theory of reality builds a bridge between matter, mind, and cosmos." Azarian, p.246.

"The experience of self is as real as any other conscious experience, such as pain or pleasure. Koch, p.128.

2. The experience of feeling. Not mere reflexive response, but feeling. Sentience.

"Self-awareness, or self-consciousness, is the subjective experience of one's own desires and emotions." Koch, p.37.

---

3. Internal dialogue.

"Its most prominent feature is a voice inside your head, though not everyone has such a voice. ...This 'I,' with its incessant silent speech, chattering about ten times faster than were you to speak aloud, plays an increasingly dominant role as you grow into adulthood." Koch, p.37.

---

4. The ability to visualize or imagine alternative scenarios, future and past.

"[C]onscious creatures really can control their own destiny by selecting the future that is consistent with their long-term goals from a menu of possible options." Azarian, p.206.

"A higher level of self-modeling, also associated with the prefrontal cortex, allows humans to simulate themselves in a seemingly infinite variety of scenarios. With a sufficiently sophisticated global workspace comes the power of imagination, which enables us to play with the mental model of the world that evolution and adaptive learning have built up in our brains. We can travel back and forward in time in our mind... ."

Azarian, p.242.

---

5. The perception of making choices, decisions, of agency.

"We must not confuse basic agency (being alive) with consciousness (being aware), because you can have agency without consciousness. Free will, on the other hand, requires consciousness, though you can be conscious without having free will." Azarian, p.207.

"[T]hese machines will never be sentient, no matter how intelligent they become. Furthermore, ... they will never possess what we have: the ability to deliberate over an upcoming choice and freely decide." Koch, p.20.

"Other experiences associated with self include agency ('I made the decision') and ownership ('it was my finger that pulled the trigger')." Koch, p.38.

Some, but not all, of these require or are assisted by language.

Koch emphasizes that subjective experiences are individual and unique. I am sure that that is true, but I think that he tries to make too much of it.

"Because we only know our own idiosyncratic view of reality, we take it for granted and assume that everyone experiences the same, although many know, in an abstract way, that our experienced realities differ in ways both small and large." Koch, p.162.

"The frequently asked question 'What is the real color of the dress' doesn't have an 'objective' answer, as color is a construct of the mind of the beholder." Koch, p.53.

"[T]here is vast genetic and developmental diversity among the eight billion people living on planet Earth, reflected in the astonishing diversity of their brains and their ways of experiencing the world. ...[W]e take reality as given and implicitly assume that everyone experiences the same, when in fact few do." Koch, pp.56, 59.

"Because we only know our own idiosyncratic view of reality, we take it for granted and assume that everyone experiences the same, although many know, in an abstract way, that our experienced realities differ in ways both small and large." Koch, p.162.

There must be very considerable commonality among human experiences to permit the emergence and evolution of societies and cultures. We may be unable ever to know what it feels like someone else, but we can have a pretty good idea. And, of course, through communication and the arts, we develop stronger and stronger understandings. But, you never know, not for sure.

"IIT"

"[T]he brain is just an amazingly complex set of interlocking dumb mechanisms causally interacting with each other. **How can conscious feelings arise from mere mechanisms?**"

Koch, p. 74 (emphasis added).

Koch and Azarian both trumpet the contributions of "integrated information theory" to our understanding of consciousness. I am unable to grasp the argument.

Koch explains:

"This starting point is what makes integrated information theory (IIT) so different from contemporary theories that start with the brain and then seek to squeeze the juice of consciousness from it using computational functionalism. IIT **starts with consciousness**, not with the brain."

...

"Besides the reasonable assumption that there are persistent objects outside my experience, integrated information theory presupposes that things exist to the extent they have cause-effect power.

"Something that cannot make a difference to anything or be influenced by anything is causally impotent. It can be disregarded from the point of view of existence.

...

"The phenomenal properties of an experience—its quality or how it feels—correspond **one-to-one to the physical properties of the intrinsic cause-effect structure unfolded from the underlying substrate**.

...

"All **quality is a structure**, not a function, a process, or a computation. One implication is that consciousness is **non-algorithmic**; it is not (Turing) computable."

Koch, pp.89, 92, 93, 100-101, 101 (emphasis added).

I am fine with the first few propositions, but I stumble over the assertions about structure and substrate. What are they and how do they explain consciousness, which certainly seems more like a process than a structure? Koch continues:

"The critical difference between brains and digital computers is at the hardware level...—...where action potentials are
relayed to tens of thousands of recipient neurons ... .[T]he
integrated information of digital computers is negligible."

Koch, p.20.

"The substrate of the mental is the neocortex and allied satellite
structures, sited like a crown on top of the brain, just underneath its
protective skull." Koch, p.114.

So, the key is in the unique intricate interconnections (sometimes
called the connectome) that enable an integrated response incorporating inputs from numerous different regions of the brain. Okay, but how
does that astonishing integration occur? As we often find in science, insights achieved reveal phenomena even more wonderous than that with
which we began the investigation.

Actually, the key is in the integration of disparate pieces of information into a single coherent "picture." Like a television screen; a million
pixels, none of which even hints at the image on the screen. But, we
see a picture—the integrated whole. Yet, absent the viewer, is there an
image or only a million pixels? Clearly, it is us watching the television
that performs the integration. The same with consciousness. The inter-
connection of thousands of individual inputs at a single point is not
sufficient. Something needs to perform the integration, the interpretation or translation, of the totality of the inputs. So, we still do not have
the answer.

The originator of the theory says this:

"Each experience ... is **a unique shape** made of integrated information—a shape that is maximally irreducible—the shape of understanding. And it is the only shape that's really real—the most real thing there is."

Tononi, Preface (emphasis added).

We get some insight into what is meant by structure. But, that does not answer the question.

The science commentator Bobby Azarian sets out the question clearly and attempts an answer.

"**Why does the global synchronous firing of certain networks of neurons create a subjective field of experience, according to Tononi's theory?** Because the brain is not just processing information, but integrating information into a unified whole. Just like a computer, the brain stores and processes information, but it is how that information is shared or distributed throughout the brain network that gives rise to our rich and vivid conscious experience. ...Inside the brain, there are many different things going on in distant places. Yet, somehow we perceive it all as one unified conscious experience. Thanks to integrated information theory, we are now beginning to understand how the perceptual binding of independently processed features happens mathematically.

...

"[T]he brain generates conscious experience when co-ordinated global activity emerges from the local electrical interactions of billions of neurons—the synchronous firing of those neurons integrates information from multiple processing streams into a single field of experience. ...Feedback loops running from the thalamus to the cortex ... integrate information and bind features into a cohesive perceptual landscape. ...**Without feedback, the brain still functions as a physiological organ controlling autonomic functions, but consciousness fades into nonexistence.**"

Azarian, pp. 200, 231 (emphasis added).

But, I am unsatisfied.

He says: "The mind can move things around in a paradox-free manner because it is not an immaterial entity as once thought; it is **a cybernetic control unit** that can steer itself toward goals that keep it in existence." *Id.*, p.234 (emphasis added). This statement does not really help. The metaphor reflects what happens, which we already know, not how it happens, the open question.

And, "It seems more appropriate to say that minds are an emergent property of systems that are configured to process and integrate information." *Id.*, p.241. Back to emergence. The idea is almost irresistible. But, that label does not explain how it happens. It also requires an acceptance of "downward causation" where the higher level state resulting from the combination of lower level building blocks can cause changes in those building blocks. (This concept is discussed elsewhere. *See Imaginings*, pp.58-6, 63-71.) However, it does provide an answer to one fundamental question—how does the immaterial cause behavior of material things. The properties of the emergent consciousness are material things.

Koch provides an interesting discussion of fetal development of human consciousness. Subject to various caveats and qualifications, he hypothesizes that it goes like this:

- "[T]he second-trimester fetus has rudimentary behavioral capacities, such as withdrawal from painful stimuli ... called nociceptive responses, that adults show without any conscious awareness."
- "The birth of neurons, called neurogenesis, starts around the fifth week and is largely completed by the end of the sixteenth week."
- "[N]eocortical neurons of a fetus are not properly wired up to receive any peripheral signals until about the thirtieth week."
- "Based on the way these circuits develop, peripheral pain signals can trigger reflexes but fail to ring the consciousness alarm until well into the third trimester."
- "[T]he fetus—floating in its own isolation tank, connected to the placenta that pumps blood, nutrients, and hormones into its growing body and brain, and suffused by sedation-promoting substances—is asleep."
- "Does a fetus dream while in active sleep? If so, what would a fetus, who is a *tabula rasa*, a blank slate in terms of life memories, dream of? ...My hunch is that the fetus does not dream in the way you and I dream. But it is difficult to know for certain."
- "A third-trimester fetus is unlikely to distinguish itself from the world; it is still egoless. The extent to which it has a primitive bodily awareness, such as pleasant sensations associated with warmth and nourishment through the placenta or painful ones, is at this stage impossible to ascertain. But it cannot be ruled out."
- "Things transform abruptly during the dramatic and highly stressful events attending natural, vaginal birth. The fetus wakes up and is forced from the only home it has ever known into

an alien world. A powerful surge of noradrenaline from the locus coeruleus deep in the brainstem ... and the cessation of sedation... ."

- "Self-awareness and silent, inner speech develop much later. Just like dreaming, these are complex cognitive processes linked to linguistic processing that take years to mature, with boys usually delayed with respect to girls."

Koch, pp. 28, 28-29, 29, 30, 31, 32, 171.

The curious thing is that when Koch gets to his integrated information theory, he expounds a view that finds causal capability or consciousness in the embryo.

"[A]n eight-week-old embryo is clearly alive but not conscious." Koch, p.171.

But,

"If an organism, such as the neural net of a jellyfish, satisfies the above five postulates, it feels-like-something. Its experience will likely include a sense of hunger, pain and primordial fear when attacked by predators, and bodily feelings of undulating in the sea—perhaps not too dissimilar from the experiences of a third-trimester fetus... ." Koch, pp.103-104.

"Provided the system has some itsy-bitsy intrinsic causal power, it will feel-like-something." Koch, p.104.

"Indeed, it may be that every organism on the tree of life feels-like-something, is sentient, although its phenomenal content may take a primitive form unrecognizable to us." Koch, p.123.

Azarian cites this conclusion as the fatal defect in the theory as an explanation of consciousness—it is missing a final step. Azarian asserts that that final step is the introduction of self reference. The mental models of reality begin to incorporate the self.

"Taken to its logical conclusions, integrated information theory says that any system that has any amount of *phi* at all should possess some degree of conscious experience and should have some degree of causal power." Azarian, p.202.

It certainly seems that a theory of consciousness needs to include the phenomenon of self awareness, but I doubt that we get there merely by introducing the self as another character in the model. Indeed, one of the striking features of consciousness, in contrast to dreams, is the unique and central role played by the self.

II.

Race and Racism: Origins?

"'No one was white before he/she
came to America,'James Baldwin once said.".
..."They **don't become black** until
they go to America ... ," she said.

...

"It was in the making of the New World
that humans were set apart
on the basis of what they looked like ...
and ranked to form a caste system
based on **a new concept called race**."

Isabel Wilkerson
Caste: The Origins of Our Discontents,
pp.50, 52, 52 (emphasis added).

A common theme in recent books on racism, such as Isabel Wilkerson's *Caste,* is the claim that the centrality of race in human affairs is a distinct product of North America. Interesting. However, I have not seen very persuasive evidence of the claim.

Of course, the importance of "Black" is, in fact, the result of events in the United States, events that occurred over the past 50 years. But, that is not what is being referenced here. Prior to 1970, the word was Negro or colored.

It seems that no one has written that book.

The thesis would be that the concept of race emerged to assure the dominance of whites over Blacks in America. So, was the concept of an inferior race embodied in that word a uniquely American construct? I have not tried to research the matter, so I only offer references to some well known facts.

Consider the following:

1. The word Negro apparently derived from Spanish and/or Portuguese meaning "black" and was used with respect to persons from Africa.

2. The treatment of black as evil or bad relative to white appears in Shakespeare's Othello written in 1602. ("Even now, now, very now, an old black ram. Is tupping your white ewe. Arise, arise! Awake the snorting citizens... .")

"After seeing it performed in 1786, ... [Abigail Adams] wrote to her sister, 'I could not separate the African color from the man, nor prevent that disgust and horror which filled my mind every time I saw him touch the gentle Desdemona.'

...

"Though, as with Abigail Adams, many white Americans may have seen the play through a predominantly racial lens, there is little evidence that 18th-century U.S. productions of Othello sparked widespread public debate on race."

Andrew Carlson, "Not Just Black and White: 'Othello' in America," *Theatre History*, December 27, 2016.

---

3. Some references to "Reports on Africa and Africans from the 16th century":

"Best, an English chronicler, includes the following anecdote in his 1578 book A True Discourse of the Late Voyages of Discouerie:

'I myself have seene an Ethiopian as black as cole brought into Englande, who taking a fair Englishe woman to Wife, begatte a Sonne in all respectes as blacke as the father was, although England were his native Countrey, and an English woman his Mother: whereby it seemeth this blacknesse proceedeth rather of some naturall infection of that man, which was so strong, that neyther the nature of the Clime, neyther the good complexion of the Mother concurring, coulde any thing alter, and therefore we cannot impute it to the nature of the Clime.'

"Iago, in his attempt to disempower Othello, depicts him as bestial and animal-like, drawing on the cultural misconception of Africans as monstrous and subhuman. This misconception appeared as the result of 16th century literature on Africans, such as Konrad Lykosthenes' 1581 book 'The doome warning all men to the iudgemente... .'"

Mari Rooney, "'Fall'n in the Practice of a Slave': Racial Ideology and Villaney in Shakespeare's Othello," *bu.ed/writingprogram*, August 10, 2018.

The thesis of this student's essay is that Shakespeare intended Othello to be a rebuke of sixteenth century racial prejudices, with the villain being the racist and the tragic noble the black Moor. That makes sense, but is only suggestive of the existence of sixteenth-century racism in England.

---

4. The stigma of darker skin color was prevalent in India (and, elsewhere). Wilkerson, *Caste*, pp.176-7.

"[T]he heartbreak of the Indian fixation on skin color, which was caste within caste, and the hatred of darker Indians, who tend to be lower caste but not always, and how they suffer for this accident of fate, as do ... other people of color ... in other parts of the world." *Id.*, p.176.

---

5. The category of Caucasian as a "race" arose in Germany at the end of the eighteenth century.

"[T]he use of the term Caucasian to label people descended from Europe is a relatively new and arbitrary practice in human history. The word was not passed down from the ancients but rather sprang from the mind of a German professor of medicine, Johann Friedrich Blumenbach, in 1795." *Id.*, p.65.

---

6. Discrimination or mistreatment based on "race" was a theme of *The Merchant of Venice* by Shakespeare. ("If you tickle us do we not laugh? If you poison us do we not die? And if you wrong us shall we not revenge?")

7. The early official U.S. Census did not categorize people by race.

"In 1790, the race categories were free whites, free others, and slaves. By 1850, ... the census added a new category, 'Mulatto.'" *Id.*, p.400.

---

8. The discriminatory attitudes and conduct in America were not limited to Blacks. Germans, Irish, Italians, Chinese and Jews, in turn and among other groups, were similarly stigmatized.

"Twenty-five years before the American Revolution, Benjamin Franklin worried that, with its growing German population, Pennsylvania would 'become a Colony of Aliens, who will shortly be so numerous as to Germanize us, instead of our Anglifying them, and will never adopt our Language or Customs any more than they can acquire our Complexion.'" *Id.*, p.122.

Wilkerson quotes an acquaintance:

"'Africans are not black,' she [a Nigerian-born playwright at a talk in London] said. 'They are Igbo and Yoruba, Ewe, Akan, Ndebele. They are not black. They are just themselves.'"

Id., p.53.

This assertion is rather silly. In a region where virtually all of the population is Black, no one identifies their neighbors as Black. Instead, they utilize other distinguishing characteristics to discriminate. African Blacks in several countries have engaged in conduct toward other groups of Blacks that resembles Nazi Germany much more closely than it does the United States at any point in our history. (Of course, we find genocide on all continents with substantial populations.)

There is reason to believe that it is overly simplistic or, even, false to characterize racism as a distinctly American phenomenon.

But, what about slavery?

We start with the fact that in English North America, slavery was an economic institution. It's reason for being was economic—the New World had an amazing abundance of land and other natural resources and a scarcity of labor and farming skills.

> "The strengths of African workers became their undoing. British colonists in the West Indies, for example, saw Africans as 'a civilized and relatively docile population,' who were 'accustomed to discipline,' and who cooperated well on a given task. Africans demonstrated an immunity to European diseases, making them more viable to the colonists than were the indigenous people the Europeans had originally tried to enslave."

Id., p.42.

Plantation slavery developed according to a logic inherent in the institution. Slaves were to be property, so a legal structure was needed to define and protect the rights in that property. Slavery depended on coercion, so rules concerning and providing coercion were needed. The circumstances in English North America, unlike in some other regions allowed slaves generally to live through their reproductive years, so the status of children had to be specified. The issue was different from that of primogeniture. The children had economic value. Looking to the mother made economic sense. Maternity was unambiguous; if the mother "belonged" to someone who provided room and board for her, the child would be expected to follow.

In the earliest days, slavery was reconciled with Catholicism on the premise that the people enslaved were not Christian. Thus, in many colonies, slaves who converted were freed under the law. However, as the colonies became increasingly dependent on slave labor, economics won out over the rather wishy-washy religious rationale. By the beginning of the Eighteenth Century, most colonies had enacted laws providing that baptism or conversion were not grounds for manumission. Even the practice in states after the Civil War of leasing convicted men to private enterprises was similarly a product of greed, profit seeking and corruption, tragically facilitated by the vulnerability of Blacks in transit.

My point here is not that slavery was not immoral, but that a case can be made that race was incidental to the institution and neither the cause nor driving force. One could leave out race and expect a similar result.

So, then, what is the origin of race and race-consciousness? I do not know, but it does not appear to be in English North America. The reality is much more complex than Wilkerson would like to have us believe.

CHAPTER 5

Puzzles Unsolved

I.

The Feeling of Color

I previously discussed a hypothetical proposed by Australian philosopher Frank Jackson in the 1980s and compared the conclusions reached by Sean M. Carroll, (*The Big Picture: On the Origins of Life, Meaning, and the Universe Itself* (2016), p.353) and Nicholas Humphrey (*Sentience: The Invention of Consciousness* (2023), pp.96-8).

The hypothetical:

"Mary is a neuroscientist who knows everything there is to know about the color red, but she has never seen anything red. One day, Mary sees red.

"Does she learn anything new?"

I criticize the views expressed by each of the two scientists.

Then, I conclude:

> "We should just admit that Mary had a new experience and learned something. The question to address is what are the implications?"

Not much of an answer.

I find that I actually do have an opinion about the hypothetical, because I have strong feelings about color.

When I could no longer ride on the stairlift and had become confined to my power wheelchair, I had to move completely to ground floor, already equipped with ramps. So, my ground floor library, with the construction of a "rollin" shower nearby, became my sleeping room. It is a deep burgundy in color. In and around the hundreds of books, I have had hung some 15 oil paintings, mainly of clowns and still lifes, all full of color. I love the richness, the vividness and, during the day, the play of sunlight coming through the windows. I find that the colors produce in me a sense of calm, a feeling of security. Examing the paintings brings cheerfulness. My world becomes larger. I am happy.

How does it happen?

By association? The triggering of memories? The release of hormones? Something else?

I know that the colors are the consequences of differing frequencies of light, that there is nothing "there," at least nothing that resembles what I perceive. At some level, I find that virtually inconceivable My reality and that of the physicists hardly overlap. But, my world requires a conscious observer, one who experiences. Indeed, my world is that of conscious observation, the assimilation of sensory data and the output of my conscious and unconscious mind.

Yes, Mary learns something (unless you artificially define "learn" to apply only to certain types of knowledge). Mary learns what red feels like.

"'You see,' said Alturi, 'even if we understood completely the mechanisms for distinguishing among the colors, down to the most niggling detail, we would still fail to understand why, alongside the nerve cells in the visual parts of the brain, which slavishly perform their task—the task of distinguishing among colors—and use those distinctions to guide our behavior, why alongside all of this there should also exist a conscious experience of color—an I who sees in front of himself, vividly, a red apple, or a blue sky. No matter how I program the machine, what steps I force it to follow, I cannot see how it could see the same way I see,' said Alturi. 'It could perhaps behave like me, but I just cannot see how it would experience anything at all.'

Giulio Tononi, *Phi: A Voyage from the Brain to the Soul* (2012), p.122.

Curiously, the mechanisms through which Mary and I perceive the colors are well understood. I quote a lengthy passage from a former theoretical physicist turned writer detailing what happens.

"Each particle of light ends its journey in the eye upon meeting a retinene molecule, consisting of 20 carbon atoms, 28 hydrogen atoms, and 1 oxygen atom. ...In its dormant condition, each retinene molecule is attached to a protein molecule and has a twist between the eleventh and fifteenth carbon atoms. But when light strikes it ... the molecule straightens out and separates from its protein.

"...Triggered by the dance of the retinene molecules, the nerve cells, or neurons, respond. ...This change in flow of electrically charged atoms produces a change in voltage... . After a distance of a fraction of an inch, the electrical signal reaches the end of the neuron, altering the release of specific molecules, which migrate a distance of a hundred-thousandth of an inch until they reach the next neuron... ."

...

"In another few thousandths of a second, the electrical signals reach the ganglion neurons, which bunch together in the optic nerve at the back of the eye and carry their data to the brain. Here, the impulses race to the primary visual cortex, a highly folded layer of tissue about a tenth of an inch thick and two square inches in area, containing one hundred million neurons in half a dozen layers. The fourth layer receives the input first, does a preliminary analysis, and transfers the information to neurons in other layers."

...

"At every stage, each neuron receives signals from a thousand other neurons, combines the signals—some of which cancel one another out—and dispatches the computed result to a thousand-odd other neurons."

Alan Lightman, *Probable Impossibilities: Musings on Beginnings and Endings* (2021), pp.87, 88.

Pretty incredible.

But, nothing in this long description begins to tell us how or why the colors evoke deep emotional responses in me. Lightman admits as much. His description quoted above is of a man who sees an attractive woman.

He concludes:

"What is not known is why, after about a minute, the man walks over to the woman and smiles."

Id., p.90.

"Explaining color to achromats [persons who cannot see color] is impossible, for colors are more than a semantic label attached to surfaces. It feels-like-something to see the colors of a fluttering flag or the setting sun. Colors, like any other experience, have what is called a quale (plural qualia), a unique feeling that makes seeing orange quite different from seeing purple and radically different from smelling garlic or touching a wet towel."

Christof Koch, *Then I Am Myself the World: What Consciousness Is and How to Expand It* (2024), p.57.

These comments have been addressed to sight, to seeing colors; but, they apply to all of the senses. You could know everything about sound, but you will experience music. The same for taste and smell.

Perhaps, touch or feel is an outlier. I need to think about that.

II.

The 2024 Election

"US culture is an incubator of 'extrinsic values'."

George Monbiot
"To beat Trump, we need to know
why Americans keep voting for him.
Psychologists may have the answer,"
The Guardian, 29 January 2024.

"Psychologists may have the answer," but George Monbiot does not. Indeed, I find this article rather silly. An extreme oversimplification, obviously, but the extrinsic/intrinsic distinction is not relevant to the issues with which we should be concerned. This columnist undoubtedly relishes a theory that makes Trumpism "a" (or, perhaps, "the") end stage of unfettered capitalism and free markets, but he fails to explain why ambitious, selfish, successful people or, alternatively, unsuccessful tycoon wannabes would be drawn to vote for Trump. Arguably, they would be more tolerant of his character flaws, but that is different from supporting him.

Monbiot is suggesting that persons consumed by extrinsic values are or will become like Trump, but simple observation shows that not to true. Separately, does an alleged significant shift from intrinsic values toward extrinsic values, if it has occurred (which I doubt), appear to capture what is happening today?

Not for me.

I think something significant has occurred. It is not an increase in ambition and greed or in materialism; it is the emergence of self obsession, self worship and self indulgence, reflected in the selfie, social media and reality TV. This disease has spread rapidly and broadly, a global pandemic. Gone is respect for duty, restraint, humility, sacrifice and service. This change has made a Donald Trump tolerable if not acceptable and, even, if not desirable. But, why the votes?

I found myself spiraling downward emotionally during the last few months of 2023. I was increasingly distressed by world events (which have only gotten worse), but I realize that I was particularly knocked down by the political situation in the United States. It was causing me anguish and creating a feeling of hopelessness, of sinking out of control.

Curiously, I am now much better. What has changed?

I think two things, one my conception of what is happening and the other a decision about what I will do. First, I have accepted that tens of millions of people want to vote for Donald Trump. I cannot under-stand why or how. It is truly shocking to me, to the core. But, I refuse to villainize those people. I think one must presume the good faith of voters (absent clear evidence of corruption or fraudulent conspiracy). And, I recognize that a commitment to free elections requires a gracious (or, at least, civil) acceptance of the results. But, I am disappointed.

(And, I cannot help but feel disgusted by the decisions of failed candidates to endorse Trump. I consider that to be the elevation of personal ambition far ahead of the public interest.)

Second, I resolved that, henceforth, I shall vote for, and only vote for, candidates who I think are suitable for the office and likely to do a good job. No more selecting "the lesser evil" nor voting against someone. I know that I will, in the process, arguably "waste" my vote. However, I do not consider it a waste. It is a protest. It is more constructive and positive than just not voting. (I am increasingly irritated by negative campaigning. I would like to hear why someone should be elected for reasons other than to block someone else's election. Yet, I know what we will hear from the candidates and pundits.)

It appears that we will experience an unprecedented election, one in which each party nominates the one candidate that the other party's candidate might be able to defeat—likely, almost any moderate Democratic (or Republican) could defeat Trump, and almost any moderate Republican (or Democrat) could defeat Biden. Indeed, one might summize that each party is resisting the selection of a strong candidate for fear of inciting the other party to select an even stronger candidate. Remarkable. And, disappointing.

I am not seriously suggesting that these are the actual motivations of anyone, but the situation reflects a kind of paralyzing equilibrium that may lead to a most unfortunate electoral contest in November. The egos of both Trump and Biden desperately want to be President again. Trump's avid supporters will give him the nomination; Biden's position as incumbent will give him the nomination.

"If Mr. Schumer and other Democratic power-brokers truly thought ... that Mr. Trump would abrogate the Constitution and bring about an autocracy... , they wouldn't give him a boost for the sake of marginal political gain. They are willing to give him a boost, again and again, because they don't believe their own predictions about a second Trump term. They rather enjoyed his first one."

Barton Swaim, "Why Democrats Can't Quit Trump," *WSJ.com*, March 31, 2024.

I blame Biden. As he made clear in his State of the Union speech February 7, 2024, he is determined to pursue reelection with no offerings and no overtures to the other side or, even, to the middle. He is oblivious to his limitations and vulnerabilities. His arrogance and self-centeredness are real dangers. I cannot blame Trump any more than I would blame a rabid animal. Perhaps, Biden cannot help himself either. I do not really comprehend pathologies.

Maybe Robert Sapolsky is right—that no one should be blamed for their actions; that we are all just slaves to our destinies. *See Determined: A Science of Life without Free Will* (2023). If so, then

> "I commend[] mirth, because a man
> hath no better thing under the sun,
> than to eat, and to drink, and to be merry."

Ecclesiastes 8:15.

But, I cannot really believe that. It is contrary to my most fundamental instincts. We must be (or, at least, believe that we are) are responsible for our actions and decisions.

I think history will judge Biden harshly.

"[If only] Mr. Biden had found the wisdom and self-restraint to do as he originally implied—*i.e.*, free himself from frantic careerist calculation and embrace the role of one-term president. (After all, careerist calculation looks especially shabby from a politician visibly past retirement age and ready for the pasture.) But credit Team Biden with one... .They rightly saw that any Republican nominee not named Trump might give voters rein to vent their throw-the-bum-out instinct. To avoid Jimmy Carter's fate, they would make sure voters could only rid themselves of Mr. Biden by surrendering to Mr.

Trump. This bet may yet pay off for Mr. Biden, if not the country. Should he lose, it also sets him up to rocket to the bottom of the presidential standings, permanently displacing the luckless James Buchanan as America's worst president."

Holman W. Jenkins, Jr., "EV Tariffs and the Inanity of Bidenism," *WSJ.com*, May 14, 2024.

If the only issues were domestic, I could still be pretty relaxed. We survived Trump once, we should be able to again. Our system of checks and balances is probably stronger today than five years ago. We will likely survive Biden's domestic policies too; although, inflation and the budget deficit will challenge our future, four more years will have a *de minimise* additional adverse impact. The problem is foreign affairs. The world seems more dangerous now than at anytime I can remember (and, I remember fallout shelters and crawling under our school desks as part of emergency drills). Neither likely candidate is even remotely up to the task ahead. I think age alone disqualifies both; although, their temperaments and characters are totally unsuitable, regardless of age.

But, what can I do except worry?

I will probably need to "write in" someone.

Now, I have to figure out how to do so without hands that work. But, here in February, November seems so far away.

III.

A New Racism?

This is a troubling time for my generation. The year I was born, President Truman ordered the desegregation of the U.S. Armed Forces (July 26, 1948, Executive Order 9981, creating the President's Committee on Equality of Treatment and Opportunity in the Armed Services and mandating the desegregation of the U.S. military). Also, "[i]n 1948, the entire federal criminal code was dramatically rewritten, further clarifying the laws against involuntary servitude. ...Finally, in 1951, Congress passed even more explicit statutes, making any form of slavery in the United States indisputably a crime." Douglas A. Blackmon, *Slavery by Another Name: The Re-Enslavement of Black Americans from the Civil War to World War II* (2008), p.381.

The background of my childhood included the Civil Rights marches and demonstrations across the South; of my teens, the powerful image of Assistant U.S. Attorney General Nickolas deB. Katzenback nose to nose with a defiant George Wallace at the entrance to the University of Alabama in 1963 and the enactment of The Civil Rights Act of 1964 ending Jim Crow throughout the country. In the year I turned 60, the country elected its first Black president.

Nick Katzenback was a big man with a large head but not what one would call a physical person. When I knew him almost 20 years later, his most striking characteristics (besides his intelligence) were his kindness and his projection of absolute calm.

I have lived through a very different world than had my grandfather born in 1899.

To be clear, race and racism were rather abstract, distant concepts for me growing up. My grandparents were quite prejudiced, but toward Catholics. Actually, not Catholics, but the Catholic Church. I think that one of their big concerns was that one of their grandchildren would marry a Catholic. My father had commanded a mortar platoon of Black soldiers in Italy during the war (before desegregation), but I did not know that until I was a teenager. My mother's parents became resentful when the value of their home fell, wiping out their retirement savings, as their neighborhood became integrated. My parents were apparently quite open minded.

However, in college and, then, at the law firm, I observed and, as hiring partner, participated in so-called affirmative action. I thought it made sense. Society would benefit from increasing interaction among races and some individuals with strong potential would get the opportunity to prove themselves that deficient education and cultural disadvantages would otherwise have denied them. (By the way, i did not limit my exceptions based on race.) But, this was a short-term and very limited "patch," a band-aid, affecting only the most exceptional individuals. The real solution would be in addressing and reducing the deficiencies that create the disadvantages.

In any event, I entered my mature years believing, like many, that the issues of race and racism were well on the way out, really things of the past.

I retired in 2011 and lived in England from then until mid-2015. I returned to the States to discover the beginnings of the new racism. It seemed that colorblindness was no longer the "gold standard" as my generation (of, I think, all races) had believed.

Instead, we have: "Race" (as central to U.S. life and history), "White privilege","Systemic racism", "Black Lives Matter", "Reparations."

"Our country has never been colorblind. Given the lengthy history of state-sponsored race-based preferences in America, to say that anyone is now victimized if a college considers whether that legacy of discrimination has un-equally advantaged its applicants fails to acknowledge the well-documented 'intergenerational transmission of inequality' that still plagues our citizenry."

Justice Jackson's dissent, *Students for Fair Admissions v. Harvard*, 600 U.S. 181 (2023).

"[N]one of the actions we are told Black people must take if they want to 'lift themselves' out of poverty and gain financial stability ... can mitigate four hundred years of racialized plundering."

...

"At the center of those policies must be reparations. It does not matter if your ancestors engaged in slavery or if you just immigrated here two weeks ago."

Nikole Hannah-Jones, *The 1619 Project: A New Origin Story* (2021), pp.471, 472.

What the hell happened?

Over the next few years, I tried to educate myself about this new point of view. I was not very impressed and certainly not persuaded. I have written critiques of many of the books and have presented my thoughts on several of the relevant topics. Of course, the inadequacies of the arguments of the proponents do not establish the incorrectness of the proposition. So, I decided to address the issue directly.

I just read Coleman Hughes book—*The End of Race Politics: Arguments for a Colorblind America* (2024)—and I found that his straight forward presentation, generally avoiding the overblown rhetoric of those whose positions he criticizes, helped me organize my thought. (He refers to what I had characterized as the new racism as "neo-racism.") I agree with much of what Hughes has to say, but I have reservations about two of his conclusions: that the new racism is based upon retribution and that its appearance was caused by smartphones and social media.

As to the first, he is surely correct about the unfortunate consequences of the seeking of retribution (*id.*, pp.156-7), but I doubt that he is correct about the motivations behind or the goals of the "neoracist."

"[T]he law of retaliation, the principle of taking an eye for an eye, is a simplistic and outmoded way to think of justice, one that leads to interminable hatred generation after generation. ...Discriminating against white people in the present doesn't erase the injustice of discrimination against black people in the past. It doesn't decrease the sum total of injustice in the world. ...Any act of injustice adds to the sum total of injustice in the world."

Hughes, pp.120, 121, 122.

I do not know these people, so I can only guess about motivations, but I doubt that it is a desire for retribution. Hughes notes that the outspoken advocates of this view probably do not want a prompt solution, since that would curtail their career prospects (*id.*, pp.132, 176), but we need not be so cynical. However, I do think that the objective is money (rather than revenge).

Hughes argues that Blacks today are not injured by past racist practices and that income differentials today are not likely caused by discrimination (*id.*, pp.116-8). However, he does not address one of the arguments made—that Blacks would be wealthier today if their ancestors had been better off, because they would have inherited wealth. Now, that is a highly speculative argument and, whatever its merits with respect to possible statistical averages, an impossible basis on which to assert claims for individual entitlements or injury. (I discuss the "wealth gap" in another essay.) So, I agree with Hughes about the validity of claims for "reparations." Yet, that seems to be what is really at issue.

As for the second point, Hughes looks at Gallup poll results showing that people's feelings about race relationships began to turn negative in 2013 and have continued steadily down ward since. He observes that 2013 was something of a watershed moment for video phones.

"The more plausible explanation is that 2013 is about the time that a critical mass of Americans had two pieces of tech: camera-enabled smart-phones and social media. ...Neoracist ideas were able to take advantage of this development in a way that other ideas could not. ...Anything that appeals to our tribal identities, us versus them narratives, or historical grievances travels fast." *Id.*, pp.93-94.

Well, I am sure that smartphones and social media have substantially inflamed and spread the racist sentiments, but the cause?

Justice, Looting and Violence

"Why did some poor people take to the streets and others not? How to explain why some cities where conditions were wretched remained calm while others with better conditions experienced disturbances? Why do poor whites not riot?"

Steven M. Gillon, "Why the 1967 Kerner Report on Urban Riots Suppressed Its Own Expert Findings," *History.com*, June 8, 2018 (up-dated January 31, 2019).

1965 and 1967

Hughes claims that the race riots in 1965 and 1967 caused an abandonment of the "colorblind" principle.

"Why the sudden pivot away from colorblindness? The answer has to do in part with the race riots that rocked cities like Detroit and Newark in the mid-1960s—especially during the summer of 1967. Many Americans were shocked to see black people rioting at the very moment when it seemed that the civil rights movement had achieved its greatest successes. They expected that the movement's success would have the effect of quelling civil unrest, but it did just the opposite. In the resulting confusion and dismay, people lost faith in the colorblind principle."

Hughes, pp. 57-58.

I doubt that. My personal observations as a college student at the time were that the issue commanding attention was the war in Vietnam. I think that many viewed the riot in Watts in 1965 and the similar urban disturbances in 1967 as reflections of particular local conditions in a few cities and some copycat responses. The Kent State shootings on May 4, 1970, were perceived as much more of a direct threat to our way of life.

President Johnson appointed the Kerner Commission to investigate the causes of the 1967 riots. In 1968, the Commission issued its final report finding that the cause of the riots was "white racism." Curiously, when the group of social scientists engaged by the Commission provided a preliminary report, the Commission rejected it and ordered the destruction of the report. This event can be misinterpreted. As I read the materials, the project of the researchers was terminated not because of their conclusions, but because the work was taking way too long (the report was decidedly an incomplete tentative first draft) and it was likely to produce ambiguous and overly nuanced results. The Commission wanted a prompt and decisive Report, and the conclusions and recommendations were already emerging from the negotiations among the Commissioners.

"The commission's executive staff was not interested in ambiguity; it needed to produce a final document that would garner the signatures of 11 commissioners and, hopefully, gain the support of the White House. As a result, the staff ordered all copies of *Harvest* destroyed and dismissed all but one of the social scientists. Instead, the final document the commission submitted blamed the disturbances on 'white racism' and the economic disadvantage that it caused."

Gillon, "Why the 1967 Kerner Report," June 8, 2018.

The final report:

"was a provocative statement about the problems that shaped racial conditions in urban America. The report described the riots as the outgrowth of racial inequality and oppression rather than as acts of political or criminal agitation. ...[T]he commissioners devoted almost all of their attention to institutional forces, such as unemployment and housing discrimination."

Julian E. Zelizer, "Fifty Years Ago, the Government Said Black Lives Matter: The radical conclusions of the 1968 Kerner Report." *Boston Review,* May 5, 2016.

President Johnson was unhappy with the Report, presumably because it failed to praise his quite remarkable legislative accomplishments.

"President Lyndon Johnson constituted the Kerner Commission to identify the genesis of the violent 1967 riots that killed 43 in Detroit and 26 in Newark ..., while causing fewer casualties in 23 other cities. ...[I]n March 1968, the Kerner Commission ... declar[ed] white racism—not black anger—turned the key that unlocked urban American turmoil. ...'White society,' the presidentially appointed panel reported, 'is deeply implicated in the ghetto. White institutions created it, white institutions maintain it, and white society condones it.'"

Alice George, "The 1968 Kerner Commission Got It Right, But Nobody Listened: Released 50 years ago, the infamous report found that poverty and institutional racism were driving inner-city violence," *The Smithsonian*, March 1, 2018.

"President Johnson, who was facing a tough reelection campaign and struggling with whether he should even be running, was unhappy with the findings... . He felt that the report had not given sufficient credit to his Great Society for alleviating racial inequality and that it called for programs, such as higher taxes, that were politically impossible."

Zelizer, "Fifty Years Ago," May 5, 2016.

The Report was not particularly well received and had minimal impact.

"Public opinion polls ... reflect how the report's findings were received differently by white and black Americans. In mid-April, ... 53 percent of white

Americans polled rejected the commission's claim that white racism was to blame for the riots, while 58 percent of African Americans agreed with the findings. ... By a margin of 2 to 1, whites rejected the Kerner Commission's claim that organized groups were not behind the violence." *Id.*

The cancelled preliminary report was published in 2018. Robert Shellow, *The Harvest of American Racism: The Political Meaning of Violence in the Summer of 1967* (2018). "One of the original researchers later found a copy in an archive with the word 'Destroy' stamped on the cover page." *Id.*, p.vii. The preliminary report is clearly a draft in progress. One of the authors has since said "one hastily put together, underdeveloped, and, although data-rich, poorly integrated report. It was minimally analytic and did not elaborate on the general charge of racism." Shellow, *The Harvest*, p.134. The last chapter (Chapter 7), apparently authored by one person, Lou Goldberg, is completely disconnected from the prior six analytical chapters. ("Our mistake, my mistake, was to let the chapter go without a meticulous review, something I belatedly realized at the time." *Id.*, p.121.) Yet, it was the center of most of the controversy and is what has been quoted and summarized in the subsequent commentary.

Note that the riot by a white mob in Tulsa in 1921 was directed against Blacks and black-owned businesses and property, while the later Black riots destroyed primarily Black neighborhoods. The Tulsa riot began with an armed confrontation between hundreds of Blacks and perhaps 2000 whites over a threatened lynching—a far more explosive situation than the events that sparked the 1960s riots. The white mob promptly moved to attack the prosperous Black neighborhood, presumably the source and object of white resentment. In the subsequent Black riots, the mobs attacked local businesses, presumably because they were perceived to have been exploiting the community. They were not typical race riots.

A few quite interesting observations appear in the analytical chapters:

1. The course of the disturbances was heavily influenced by strategic and tactical choices made by the police. The level of violence and property damage could probably be controlled by more sophisticated and informed approaches to crowd control.

2. The smaller disturbances had significant political content, often with specific objectives being pursued. "In a number of other cities disturbances took the form of political confrontation, in which goals and processes were more explicit, form and structure more evident." Shellow, *The Harvest,* p.28. For the major disturbances in the largest cities (Watts, Detroit and Newark), the situation was more ambiguous.

3. The actions of the rioters was directed against local businesses owned by whites and not against whites generally. "The focus of Negro antagonism in the riots is white authority and white property: mainly the police and white stores. Their antagonism is directed at white dominance over Negroes rather than at white people per se. The impulse toward indiscriminate attacks on whites has been notably absent." *Id.,* p.98.

4. The participants were predominately young 15 to 30) but otherwise reflected the Black population generally, not disproportionately consisting of the poorest or least educated residents. *Id.,* pp.54, 67, 70.

5. The disturbances were not caused by outside agitators, whether foreign or domestic, and were not particularly influenced by the more radical Black movements. "Objective examination indicates that they are very low on the list of causal factors in the recent disorders." *Id.,* p.36.

6. The participating youth typically felt alienated from their elders and excluded from political influence: "[T]he ingredients of a revolt by the militant young against their more conservative elders, a tension that had been brewing for some time... ." *Id.,* p.30.

7. "One factor that needs to be emphasized as a major source for aggressive ghetto upheavals, political rebellions, and anticipatory white responses is leadership competition within the Negro community." *Id.*, p.35.

Indeed,

"The social scientists ... found no direct relationship between poverty and rioting. Their studies had found poor African Americans were no more likely to participate in the disorders than their middle-class neighbors. Rioters were not, by all the evidence, disproportionately poor or disengaged from the communities around them. ...Those most likely to riot shared one characteristic—they had experienced or witnessed an act of police brutality."

Gillon, "Why the 1967 Kerner Report," June 8, 2018.

To me, these facts do not suggest the conclusions of the final chapter or of the actual Report. Instead, they suggest that improvement was possible through incremental reforms addressing the issues of concern and through increased civil participation by the young people as they age. The handful of large urban ghettos, however, probably would have benefited from more significant and costly intervention. Subsequent studies indicate that the disturbances tended to occur in the poorest communities and that those communities have continued to be the most impoverished.

"We show that in 1970, the first census year we have available, black neighborhoods that directly experienced riots were populated with residents that had lower incomes, lower educational levels, experienced higher unemployment, and had higher incidence of welfare usage than other black neighborhoods that were not directly affected by riots... .. ...More interesting, however, is that these level differences across riot and non-riot affected black neighborhoods persist over time... ."

Marcus Casey and Bradley Hardy, "50 years after the Kerner Commission report, the nation is still grappling with many of the same issues," *Brookings.edu*, September 25, 2018.

Fifty years later, the 1960s riots took on a different significance in some revisionist histories.

> "Black youth were organized in their liberation of goods from stores as one car would drive up and break out the windows and drive away while subsequent cars drove up to seize and load merchandise. Essentially, the burning occurred after the store was emptied. Black youth used citizens band radios and payphones to coordinate efforts.
>
> "...[I]t was inevitable given the long abuse of force by law enforcement and exploitative business practices in the city. ...**Black youth engaged in urban rebellion to dispense retaliatory violence.** One teenage girl was quoted as shouting, 'White men, you started all this the day you brought the first slave to this country.'"

M. Keith Claybrook, Jr., "Remembering, Rethinking, and Renaming the Watts Rebellion," *Black Perspectives [AAIHS]*, August 13, 2021 (emphasis added).

This commentary suggests two different characterizations of the event—a response to particular, localized experiences of police brutality and exploitation by neighborhood merchants or, alternatively, an attack on the white race.

The 1992 L.A. Riot

"The 1980s brought rising unemployment, gang activity, drugs and violent crime to the poorer neighborhoods of Los Angeles.

...

"Early on March 3, 1991, an intoxicated parolee named Rodney King led police on a high-speed car chase.... His subsequent beating ... was caught on video... . ...All four officers were acquitted of charges.... . The response was immediate, as protesters took to the streets.

...

"The final tally for the L.A. riots included 2,000 injuries, 12,000 arrests and 63 deaths attributed to the uprising. Upwards of 3,000 buildings were burned or destroyed and 3,000 businesses were affected as part of the $1 billion in damages sustained by the city, leaving an estimated 20,000 to 40,000 people out of work."

Editors, "Los Angeles Riots," *History.com*, April 18, 2017 (updated April 20, 2021).

The O.J. Simpson Trial 1995

"It was one of those 20th-century moments when you realized race is here to stay as an unending factor, an unyielding actor in American life. White and black saw two different realities. Whites: All the evidence points to his guilt, he's one of the most admired men in America, race isn't the story here. Blacks: This is what you do to black men, you railroad them on cooked-up evidence, there's plenty of room for doubt.

It showed in some new and unforgettable way the divided country. "

Peggy Noonan, "America in the Age of O.J. Simpson: His case gave rise to a new kind of fame and left Americans of all races cynical about the law," *WSJ.com*, April 11, 2024.

Black Lives Matter 2013

Systemic or institutional racism was being discussed by some social scientists in the late 2000s (2007-2009) but it became widely discussed only in the mid-2010s (2013-2015). Critical Race Theory arose in law schools in the 1980s but did not get much public attention until the 2010s.

"Critical Race Theory was first developed by legal scholars in the 1970s and '80s following the Civil Rights Movement. It was, in part, a response to the notion that society and institutions were 'colorblind.' CRT holds that racism was not and has never been eradicated from our laws, policies, or institutions, and is still woven into the fabric of their existence." *The Legal Defense Fund.*

Black Lives Matter was formed in 2013 in response to the acquittal of Trayvon Martin's murderer..

"Black Lives Matter Global Network Foundation, Inc. is a global organization in the US, UK, and Canada, whose mission is to eradicate white supremacy and build local power to intervene in violence inflicted on Black communities by the state and vigilantes."

"Black Lives Matter is an ideological and political intervention in a world where Black lives are systematically and intentionally targeted for demise. It is an affirmation of Black folks' humanity, our contributions to this society, and our resilience in the face of deadly oppression."

Black Lives Matter Website.

More Violence

Campus protests erupted in 2015.

"The passion that ousted the heads of the University of Missouri after protests over racial discrimination on campus is spreading to other colleges across the country, turning traditional fall semesters into a period of intense focus on racial misunderstanding and whether activism stifles free speech." Anemona Hartocollis and Jess Bidgood, "Racial Discrimination Protests Ignite at Colleges Across the U.S." *The N.Y. Times,* November 11, 2015.

So,

The change to which I am referring is the movement toward blaming not past wrongdoings, but current circumstances, with approbation placed on a racial group of today, in this case, white Americans, and the conclusion that that group is morally inferior, unworthy. That is racist.

The argument against colorblindness and in favor of race-based policies (and politics) seems to be based upon five untruths and two highly debatable beliefs.

The falsehoods are that: (i) any racial disparity is the result of racial discrimination, (ii) the two hundred year struggle against slavery and, then, racial discrimination was conducted almost exclusively by Blacks, (iii) all whites enjoy a privileged position in American society, (iv) little progress has been made by Black Americans and (v) there is little Blacks themselves can do to improve their position in the American society or economy.

The questionable propositions are that (i) more discussion about and focus on race is good and (ii) discrimination against whites and white values will benefit Blacks.

The five falsehoods are factual propositions as to which there are substantial empirical evidence of their incorrectness and little if any evidence in support. The two presumptions are more value judgments than factual statements, so they are debatable. Now, the human appeal of this viewpoint is pretty obvious. It absolves one of blame for the past, denies any responsibility for the future, provides a clear scapegoat, grants permission to hate and to act badly, makes one the center of attention and strengthens one's bargaining position and provides the possibility of windfall gains. It had to be pretty tempting, when the opportunity presented itself.

When did the change occur and what was the cause? As for the timing, one would need to identify a standard by which to decide that a change has occurred. Opinions are altered by experience and as a result of persuasion and, sometimes, through calculation. I suspect that the new racism emerged when it became clear that white guilt was a more potent tool than violence.

"We are stuck in a vicious cycle of
appeasement by one side
and goalpost shifting by the other."

Hughes, p.133.

CHAPTER 6

Opportunity Missed

I.

Reconstruction/Jim Crow

Without doubt, the circumstances immediately following Emancipation created a highly incendiary racial situation. Some 4 million people who, and most of whose parents and grandparents, had known nothing but slavery were set out on their own. The Federal government, struggling to win the War had no plans for how this historically unprecedented event could be managed. So, these 4 million people with few resources and little relevant training were just set loose.

Starting early in the century, there had been considerable discussion about the possible colonization of some remote region with freed slaves. The idea germinated the American Colonization Society and actually led to the formation of Liberia on the West Coast of Africa.

"[T]he Grain Coast was suggested as a suitable home for enslaved people in the United States after their emancipation. In 1818 two U.S. government agents and two officers of the American Colonization Society (founded 1816) visited the Grain Coast. After abortive attempts to establish settlements

---

there, an agreement was signed in 1821 between the officers of the society and local African chiefs granting the society possession of Cape Mesurado. The first group of formerly enslaved people, led by members of the society, landed in 1822... . They were followed shortly by Jehudi Ashmun, a white American, who became the real founder of Liberia. ...In 1839 Thomas Buchanan was appointed the first governor. On his death in 1841 he was succeeded by Joseph Jenkins Roberts, the colony's first Black governor, who was born free in Virginia in 1809... ."

Svend E. Holsoe, Donald Rahl Petterson, and Abeodu Bowen Jones, "Liberia", *Encyclopedia Britannica,* 14 March 2024.

It is conceivable that a massive relocation plan of that type could have been designed and implemented, but the courage demonstrated by Black Union soldiers and outspoken opposition from leading Blacks convinced Abraham Lincoln to abandon the idea.

At the same time, about 5 million white survivors in the Confederate States were effectively turned out also to fend for themselves. Their sons and fathers had been killed or maimed, their wealth had disappeared, their economies and supporting infrastructure had been destroyed and they, like their Black neighbors, faced a difficult winter with inadequate food supplies.

This fraught situation was aggravated by the discernible differences in appearance between the two groups and the legacy of economic segregation and segregation by social status. Nonetheless, through the utilization of existing skills, industriousness and luck, many whites and Blacks began to prosper.

"Since Reconstruction, Black homeownership had climbed rapidly: from about 43,000 Black families in 1870 to some 506,590 in 1910—nearly one in four Black families nationwide. America's 218,972 Black farm-owners owned more land than ever before or since: more than fifteen million acres, practically all of it in the South. ...Soon, Black business districts sprang up in nearly 'every Southern city' to sell homes, sewing machines, dressers, carpets, books, washstands, funeral policies, and more to the farmers, maids, and laborers who were joining America's consumer economy in ever greater numbers."

Dylan C. Penningroth's *Before the Movement: The Hidden History of Black Civil Rights* (2023), p.204.

"What Black families achieved during Jim Crow was astounding: from the fifteen million acres of land and $1.1 billion worth of farm property to the tuition they paid to Black churches, colleges, and more." *Id.*, p.223.

Immediately following the removal of Federal troops, the former Confederate States adopted laws that imposed the segregation and differential social status that had existed under slavery. These laws clearly inhibited the exercise of political rights by and the participation in government of Black residents, but they did not dramatically alter daily life.

Then...

Something happened during the first quarter of the twentieth century: America seemed to become actively racist. We had a practicing racist as President (Woodrow Wilson, 1913-21), we institutionalized racial categorizations (the segregation of the Federal bureaucracy under President Wilson), we experienced horrific community violence against Blacks across the states (1917-22) and we enacted radical new social assistance programs (under FDR in the 1930s) that were available mainly only to "white" Americans .

What happened? And, why did that racism take such a virulent turn? A combination of the following:

Human nature

Racism seems to be a likely consequence of in an interactive world. The distrust and suspicion of outsiders was probably an adaptive characteristic favored by evolution. People who look different or act differently may be a threat to a group's security either through violence or disease. The outsiders may also be competitors for scarce resources. In addition, when difficulties arise, humans tend to look for scape-goats. So, racial differences would be expected to be vulnerable spots in human relations, to be overcome through favorable experience and education or exacerbated by unfavorable experience and education. Of course, we must include humankind's propensity for violence, which I do not understand.

Science

We should also consider the role played by science. The social applications of Darwinism and the attention focused on eugenics cer-tainly must have had an impact on attitudes and opinions and affected discussion.

"Then science was conscripted to do the dirty work of white supremacy as social Darwinism held that race hierarchy was nature's will. Evolutionary theory and a sham science of eugenics and phrenology justified the wealth gap in the nineteenth century."

...

"[I]nstead of the Bible, white supremacists turned to Darwin. Social Darwinist theories of 'survival of the fittest' created a more virulent and hostile strand of racism than had existed under slavery. Evolution-based theories cast the racial hierarchy as an inevitable by-product of natural selection."

...

"The justification used to enforce this order was not economic. Rather, racial Darwinism convinced Americans that blacks were less-evolved humans... ."

Mehrsa Baradaran, *The Color of Money: Black Banks and the Racial Wealth Gap* (2017), pp.6, 64, 68.

"It is important to appreciate that within the U.S. and European scientific communities these ideas were not fringe but widely held and taught in universities. The report of the Eugenics meeting was the lead story in the journal *Science* on October 7, 1921, and this opening address was published, in its entirety, beginning on the first page of the issue."

Steven A. Farber, "U.S. Scientists' Role in the Eugenics Movement (1907–1939): A Contemporary Biologist's Perspective," *Zebrafish*, December 2008.

It seems that the societal response following the exposure of the Nazi atrocities was to ban the discussion of these subjects and to condemn the proponents. If this purportedly science-based view was really a significant contributor to the racist attitudes, then the most effective response would have been a science-based rebuttal. Instead, the principal effort was to crush it with morality based denunciations, successful most likely only because of the repugnance of the conduct of Nazi Germany and its position as the enemy in a brutal war.

The problem is that the failure to meet the arguments fully on the merits leaves lingering, even if unspoken, doubts. It may have been the most appropriate approach at the time, but we may (perhaps) have reached a sufficient distance to permit an analysis on the merits. By that I mean, recognize that at least some of those proponents were acting in good faith, assess the scientific merits of the theories and arguments and investigate what effects that work had on public opinion.

I note that science is still being used (or, misused) in discussions of race. Wilkerson asserts (p.66):

"The epic mapping of the human genome and the quieter, long-dreamt-of results of DNA kits ordered in time for a family reunion have shown us that race as we have come to know it is not real. ...Two decades ago, analysis of the human genome established that all human beings are 99.9 percent the same."

But, chimpanzees and bonbons share an estimated 99.8% of DNA with us; pigs, an estimated 98%. Very tiny differences in DNA can cause very dramatic differences in the length and quality of life. I do not think that science itself establishes Wilkerson's conclusion.

"[I]t is simplistic to put an actual figure on the amount of genetic material we have in common, says animal geneticist Professor Chris Moran from the University of Sydney's Faculty of Veterinary Science. ...'[I]f you compare the protein-encoding portion of our DNA we have a lot in common with a lot of mammals. ...[B]ut if you compare rapidly evolving non-coding sequences from a similar location in the genome, you may not be able to recognise any similarity at all. This means that blanket comparisons of all DNA sequences between species are not very meaningful.'"

"Do pigs share 98 per cent of human genes?" *ABC Science* [Australia], May 3, 2010.

Economic conflict

The country suffered economic hardship and severe competition for jobs at the end of WW I. There was a decided emergence of isolationist attitudes. There were increasing "class" conflicts and violence over unionization. Fluctuations in the business cycle appeared to be becoming more severe, with recessions more frequent and deeper. Industrial conflicts and violence erupted in the 1890s with the Homestead and Pullman Strikes of 1892 and 1894. Labor unrest surged in 1919. The Bolshevik Revolution of 1917 injected a new element—Communism —into the growing labor/management conflict.

The Great Migration

What has come to be called the Great Migration saw hundreds of thousands of Blacks relocate to urban centers, often in the North, from 1915 through the 1920s, perhaps a million Southern Blacks, attracted by employment opportunities that emerged during WW I. Significantly, the Black migrants located among friends, relatives, acquaintances, acquaintances of people they knew or of people who were known by people they knew. Subsequent discriminatory practices helped perpetuate segregated housing.

This was a volatile and violent period in American history.

Missed Opportunities

What was needed following the end of the war was a kind of Marshall Plan for the South like the United States undertook for Europe following WW II. Of course, there was no historical president for such a policy. The norm was for the victor to demand "reparations" from the loser, not provide him financial support.

Much of the subsequent tragedy would have been avoided had the nation undertaken to rebuild the South and provide ways forward for the destitute and displaced. The idea of "40 acres and a mule" would have been a constructive investment and should have applied to every propertyless family regardless of race.

It was the right time to implement colorblind government policies. Such an approach would not be based on the concept of compensation (for past injuries) but on relief of suffering and the creation of opportunity (the future): A wise approach given that the goal had been to preserve the Union. Everyone had an interest in the economic recovery of the South. But, human nature was not that mature. So, ...

We, as a nation, missed more such opportunities, for varied reasons.

> "There's a different narrative of race and racism in America—a story of missed opportunities to achieve a colorblind state. Key chapters in that story include the founding of our republic on the backs of slaves, the ratification of a weaker version of the Fourteenth Amendment ..., a Supreme Court decision that upheld the constitutionality of racial segregation (*Plessy*), another Supreme Court decision that fell short of affirming colorblindness (*Brown*), the betrayal of colorblindness at just the moment when the civil rights movement was enjoying its greatest success, and the rise of race consciousness... ."

Coleman Hughes, *The End of Race Politics: Arguments for a Colorblind America* (2024), p.153.

II.

[Adapted from an essay that appeared in
Politics, History and Ideology, pp.418-22.]

**"In 1866, 'civil rights' 'had meant rights of contract
and property, and the right to go to court.
By 1954, civil rights meant ending racial discrimination
on the job, at school, in voting,
and an end to lynching... ."**

Dylan C. Penningroth
Before the Movement
(2023), p.256.

Dylan C. Penningroth's *Before the Movement: The Hidden History of Black Civil Rights* (2023) was released in late September 2023. It reflects serious, labor-intensive research, lots of it. Using U.S. Census data to identify the races of litigants, the author and his assistants studied the court records of thousands of cases. The results depict real, authentic three-dimensional Black individuals who took responsibility for their lives and exercised agency, despite the formidable obstacles, some winning and some losing. Moreover, the stories are presented objectively.

Perhaps too objectively. Some advocacy would make the book more engaging. The author has prejudices and is judgemental. But, we get glimpses only. He references "the liberal individualism that this book critically examines" (p.xxviii)— but any actual critique is hard to discern. His observation that the Lincoln Republicans emphasized civil rights, and a distinction between slavery and freedom based thereon, seems to be presented as some sort of criticism, as if there were some ulterior motive or secret plan. He seems to be suggesting that developments in the twentieth-century could have been better if a different approach had been followed by Lincoln, the Republican Party and the abolitionists generally, but he does not suggest what alternatives might have been available then nor even how the outcome might have been different now.

"[D]uring the 1840s and 1850s, white northern leaders like Abraham Lincoln invented a worldview where a small bundle of prerogatives called 'civil rights' marked the fundamental difference between freedom and slavery."

...

"The Oregon dustup showed that standing up for fundamental civil rights could dovetail with a kind of least-common-denominator racial politics, and it was this combination that powered the Republican Party to the White House in 1860."

...

"In the 1850s, antislavery politicians took the vast array of practices that made up the slave system—the horrific violence, including sexual violence and family separation, the task and gang systems, the hiring and trading and bargaining and property ownership—and boiled them down to one essential idea: 'the chattel principle.' **All of slavery's cruelties, they insisted, flowed from this principle of treating a person like a thing, deprived of fundamental rights.**"

...

"[R]emember what "freedom" meant to many of those nineteenth-century Republicans: it meant the bare fact of not being a slave, the freedom to sell one's own labor."

...

"To understand why the Supreme Court's Republican justices believe that the Constitution requires government to be color-blind, we must remember how the party of Lincoln replaced the complicated world of privileges and 'community opinion' with the seductively simple principle of equal civil rights... ."

Id., pp.5, 36, 83, 86, 350.

Yet, he claims that: "This book is not a lament for the path not taken; it is not about the lost promise of private-law civil rights." *Id.*, p.349.

The foremost issue at that time was legally authorized slavery, not discrimination nor "second class" citizenship. The objective was to eliminate actual slavery, and slavery was seen as a matter of civil rights. Also, civil rights were deemed to be within the province of the Federal government. What he refers to as "social rights" were matters for the states, matters of state law.

"Slowly, the high courts converged on the idea that there were a few privileges and immunities that were more fundamental than the rest: 'natural, inherent and inalienable rights of man,' as the Supreme Court put it in 1795, beyond the power of any state to interfere with." *Id.*, p.

In fact, at that time, there was a presumption of the right to discriminate; no notion of a right not to be discriminated against. English society was based upon segregation by class, as captured by George Eliot in Middlemarch (1872), describing the society of rural England in the 1820s/1830s. The community pressures were against egalitarianism, supporting discrimination, separation and exclusivity. So to in the United States.

"The [Supreme] Court had to answer two questions in The Civil Rights Cases [1883]: which rights were 'fundamental,' and what could be done when white southerners took away those fundamental rights. [Justice Joseph] Bradley answered the first question bluntly: 'It would be running the slavery argument into the ground' to say that a cabdriver or theater owner was violating a fundamental right when he chose not to welcome someone into his taxicab or theater. Bradley was just as emphatic about the second question:

Congress could not protect people's 'social rights' with a nationwide law. It could only counteract 'state action.' If Black people were wronged by anything other than an explicitly racist state law or government official, Bradley insisted, they must go to their local courthouse and sue. Justice John Marshall Harlan's dissent revived the Black abolitionists' idea that denying any fundamental rights on the basis of race was tantamount to slavery."

Id., p.147.

There is one theme that peaks out several times, that is, that the free market system based on private property and "freedom" of contract is a sham. He even suggests, implausibly, that the Republican movement to limit slavery was part of an effort to "enslave" poor and working class whites.

"Already in the 1840s, more radical antislavery activists and politicians were going further. By widening the definition of 'slavery' to include racial discrimination against people who were not slaves, activists like Frederick Douglass and Martin Delany developed a critique of what we now call 'second-class citizenship.' ...These activists insisted that having rights did not necessarily make you free unless you had the same rights, on equal terms with everyone else. So long as Black people were not 'entirely free,' said Douglass and Delany in 1848—free 'to the full enjoyment of all those rights and privileges common to American citizens'—then they were 'slaves.'

...

"[M]ore and more white people nevertheless felt that it was money, not civil rights, that made a person free. America was becoming divided between a few rich families and 'a permanent factory population' living in bondage, they said."

Id., pp.36. 83.

Ignoring the suggestion of motivation, this is an issue discussed a bit above, in Chapter 10. At a minimum, one has to remember that until the nineteenth century, the vast bulk of mankind lived at the bare subsistence level. The first necessary objective was to create a surplus over which people could argue. Economic progress to escape the Malthusian trap requires saving, capital investment, entrepreneurship, ingenuity and risk taking.

History tells us that private profit opportunities coupled with individual freedom are the best catalysts for that behavior. Force, violence, terror and torture are effective means of acquiring power but have consistently proven incompatible with economic growth and prosperity. So, it maybe that inequalities and the appearance of exploitation are necessary to the creation of surpluses sufficient to permit significant increases in standards of living.

Without details of the arrangements Penningroth would put in place, one cannot assess whether his alternative world is viable or is simply Utopian dreaming. The disclosure of biases and reasoning invites evaluation on the merits, if the real world consequences are deemed relevant.

III.

"I became convinced that we must create a world
in which no one is super-rich—that there must
be a cap on the amount of wealth any
one person can have. I call this limitarianism."

"Occasionally, someone will agree that
inequality is a bad thing while also saying that
putting a limit on how much we can have is
too drastic a measure. Such a claim is puzzling.
How could that be the case?"

Ingrid Robeyns
Limitarianism:
The Case Against Extreme Wealth
(2024), pp.xiv, xviii.

I skimmed a review of this book that caused me mistakenly to expect sophisticated arguments and some penetrating analyses. I was intrigued, because I feel some sympathy for the general proposition being advanced. I was disappointed.

I promptly realized that the book would not be what I was looking for when I saw her definition of "super rich" and her proposed caps on individual wealth ($5 million).

I think of the "super rich" as those whose wealth enables a lifestyle that differs in kind, not just degree, from that of the upper middle class. People in the world of private jets, super yachts, large staffs, exotic cars and multiple mansions. Not that one necessarily has all of that, but could comfortably afford to. I used to view $100 million as the threshold, but times have changed. Luxury properties sell for $40 to $80 million, lottery jackpots frequently are in the hundreds of millions and now occasionally break a billion dollars. So, I would now place the threshold for being "super rich" at $500 million.

There apparently are close to 3,000 (2,668 on the Forbes list for 2022) billionaires in the world today, holding about $13 trillion. Robeyns, *Limitarianism*, p.xii. There are some 7,070 individuals with wealth of more than $500 million. Credit Suisse Research Institute, *Global Wealth Report 2022*. That group holds roughly $20 trillion out of a global total of $463.6 trillion. *Id.* (About 4%.) This is the group to which I will apply Robeyns' arguments. (There are almost 30,000 individuals with at least $100 million.)

"Dirty Money"

Robeyns argues first that certain categories of the super rich should have their wealth confiscated because it is "dirty money." Robeyns, pp.41-71. That is certainly correct with respect to dictators and oligarchs ("kleptocrats and public officials engaging in corruption ") who looted their countries, to criminals who profited through illegal activities and to those holding the proceeds of tax evasion. But, that is an objective of law enforcement, not tax policy. Whether we have significantly reduced the number of people of interest is unclear, because many of these individuals were unlikely to have been included in the initial count since their illegally obtained wealth would have been undisclosed.

However, I think she defines "dirty money" far too broadly. For example, she includes conscious tax avoidance, even though it is legal. She expresses clear distain for the "wealth-defense industry," the accountants and lawyers and bankers who provide tax advice and services. But, if one decides to use an ethical concept of "dirty "tax strategies rather than a legal definition of tax evasion, then there will be little agreement or consistency of results. Similarly, she categorizes as "dirty" wealth derived from "unethical activities" (child labor, exploitative trade, unfair labor practices, slavery) at any time in the past. Now, this is surely a standard that could never practically be implemented. But, Robeyns, has no intention that "dirty money" actually be identified. The point of her discussion is to claim that most of the wealth of the super rich (or of anyone else) is not "deserved"—that it is not something to which anyone is "entitled."

"It is rather to show that, for a significant proportion of super-rich individuals, we do not even have to ask about the negative consequences of their having so much money—a question reserved for the next two chapters. They simply should not have had that money in the first place, full stop." *Id.*, p.43.

Robeyns challenges the view that large incomes are the result of superior performance, skill, effort or ingenuity. I think that she significantly underestimates the role and impact of such individual qualities, but she also misses a fundamental point. She is correct that much of the extraordinary earnings are "economic rent," but she forgets that rents play a central role in the allocation of desired goods and services. The highest bidder gets the concert ticket, the painting, the center fielder, the quarterback, the waterfront property, the proven CEO. The alternative is to allocate by lottery or by fiat.

"It follows that the more unequal a society is, the more important it is to have government rationing rather than relying on the price mechanism." *Id.*, p.112.

Inequality is detrimental

In my earlier writings on inequality, I reviewed arguments that had been made as to why inequality was detrimental and found them strikingly unimpressive. I hoped to find something better here. Disappointment.

A principal argument is premised on the supposed bad effects of inequality, but she fails to establish any.

> "Inequality, by contrast, is only ever instrumentally important. In other words, **inequality is bad** because **it has bad consequences.** It produces **differences in social status** and thereby creates stigma and **undermines social cohesion.** It leads to the **abuse of power** and domination of the political process by the elite, which then results in unfair policies that help the rich more than the poor. It **undermines equality of opportunity.** It generates stress and has **negative effects on people's mental health.**"

Id., p.36 (emphases added).

"So here we are, with this long list of ways that wealth undermines democracy." *Id.*, p.94. But, the alleged adverse impact on social cohesion is based on a belief in the power of envy. (I discuss that last.) The alleged distortion of the political process from money is based on the mere conviction that money must make a difference. ("[I]t seems very unlikely that the funds available to lobbyists would not translate into political influence." *Id.*, p.84.) The claim of reduced opportunities is totally unsupported.

"By now, it should be abundantly clear that the economic elite have too much political power, and that they are making things worse for ordinary people." *Id.*, p.93.

"When money can be used to buy votes, those who funded the elected politician will see their interests protected in the policies that are implemented —but a large part of the costs of those policies will be borne by everyone else. Vote-buyers are, in a certain sense, free-riding on the spending of society as a whole." *Id.*, p.82.

Robeyns is highly critical of the inheritance of wealth, declaring that no one deserves to inherit. "Perhaps the most obvious case of undeserved wealth is that of inheritance. Inheritances are a significant source of extreme wealth, sometimes making individuals very rich indeed." *Id.*, p.121. Ultimately, she acknowledges that the issue in not the right to inherit, but the right to bequeath. It is the interests of the wealthholders that is at stake. (She almost, but not quite, recognizes that the concept of family is implicated.) She concludes that these interests are valid but outweighed by other considerations.

"[I]nheritances of a significant size do indeed have negative effects on other people—on society at large. They undermine equality of opportunity. They undermine social mobility. They provide negative incentives... . ...It would be a cruel society that punished this family-oriented idea of a good life in favor of the consumerist idea of one. So, in principle, the lawmaker should not disregard this aspiration. But there are other factors to take into account, such as whether the inheritance ... is so large as to threaten the common good."

Id., pp.123, 124.

Of course, she is partially correct. The matter at issue is one of degree. The bigger problem is that she fails to appreciate the impact of current estate taxes. For wealthy families in the United States, for example, the inheritance (through lifetime gifts and bequests) by family members will be taxed at 40% above a specified amount (currently about $13 million per estate). The tax can be avoided primarily only by gifts to charities. Now, one might argue for a higher or lower exemption or a higher or lower tax rate, but is error to claim that large inheritances escape tax.

Robeyns devotes the most words to the assertion that inequality contributes to climate change.

"Can we avert the climate crisis from within a system that creates such extreme wealth inequality? Can environmental safety and stability go hand in hand with the lifestyles of the super-rich?" *Id.*, p.97.

"[W]e also need to do something about extreme wealth concentration, because it is translating into lifestyles that are ecologically unsustainable." *Id.*, p.109.

Apart from her mischaracterization of the threat ("[s]cience tells us that we are turning the Earth into a place that will become uninhabitable for most humans, and indeed for many other living species" *id.*, p.112), her identification of inequality as a cause is illogical.

Greenhouse emissions are due to activities like the production of concrete and steel, the transportation of goods and flatulence of cows and sheep. How much of any of those activities are attributable to the super rich? To the top .01 or top .0001 % of the world's population? Suppose the super rich generate on average 200 tons of CO_2 per person per year and everyone else generates on average 1 ton (the 1 percent ... emit a staggering 101 tons per person per year. ... In North America, the richest 10 percent emit 69 tons of CO_2 per person each year... "*id.*, p.100). Then, the 7,000 super rich will be responsible for 1.4 million tons of CO_2 while the other 8 billion people will cause the emission of 8 billion tons.

Indeed, her own data reveals the fallacy: "In 2019, ... the global bottom 50 percent of the income and wealth distribution ... contribute ... 11.5 percent of the total emissions" (*id.*, p.100); yet, "their wealth ranges between 2 percent and 10 percent" (*id.*, p.26). Similarly, "the top 10 percent ... hold 50–70 percent of all wealth (*id.*, p.26), but "emit ... 48 percent of total global emissions" (*id.*, p.100). It seems clear that the poor are responsible for a greater percentage of greenhouse emissions than their percentage of total wealth. And, the rich are responsible for a smaller percentage than their share of total wealth—the exact opposite of the assumption on which Robeyns's argument is based. So, it is likely that a more equal distribution of income and wealth would result in greater, not lesser emissions.

(This conclusion is consistent with common experience. The lower income households invariably spend a much higher percentage of their resources on current consumption than do the richer households. The rich are responsible for more emissions per capita, but less per dollar of wealth.)

"[T]he wealth share of the bottom 50% of households in the United States increased from 1.84% to 2.65% in 2021... ." Credit Suisse Research Institute, *Global Wealth Report 2022*.

The super rich have not caused the climate change crisis. Robeyns real complaint again comes down to the envy she feels that other people must feel: "The 90 percent will resent having to make sacrifices if the 10 percent keep emitting so intensively; they will resent even more that the 1 percent are emitting many times what the 90 percent emit." *Id.*, p.115.

Envy

Interestingly, Robeyns recognizes that many people do not actually share her feelings of envy and outrage, contradicting her claim that inequality diminishes social cohesion.

That she views as an undesirable state of affairs, which she blames on "neoliberalism," a philosophical view that she condemns.

"Conceived as **a deliberate attempt by certain right-wing ideologues to dominate governance and policy-making**, this ideological revolution began gradually and was ultimately successful. It was most visible in the US under President Ronald Reagan and the UK under Prime Minister Margaret Thatcher." *Id.*, p.33 (emphasis added).

"It starts from the belief that, outside their families, humans are motivated by selfishness, and that we would all be better off if we arranged our societies accordingly. It asks us to believe that human beings are not intrinsically motivated to work hard, and so we should be extensively monitored and held accountable, even if that leads to huge bureaucracy. It asks us to believe that, in order to arrange an economy efficiently, we need to put people in competition with each other. The ... private sector can deliver services and solve problems much more effectively than the government. And it asks us to believe that, within this system, individuals should be held fully responsible for their failures and given sole credit for their success."

Id., p.34.

What is wrong about neoliberalism? The alleged source of the model and her disagreement with it. I believe, however, that a theoretical model should be assessed on its merits—the validity of its assumptions, the soundness of its inferences and the accuracy of its predictions—and not by who its proponents are. Robeyns, however, simply presumes that her readers share her biases and need no evidence or analysis.

She asks:

> "So why, then, do they not vote for more redistribution? There are many possible explanations. **One is that they believe** in the existence of social mobility—**in the American Dream**... . **Another possible explanation** was offered in the second part of the study... . The participants **dramatically underestimated how unequal the distribution of wealth in their country was.**"

Id., p.205 (emphasis added).

A third possibility, one she does not recognize, is that many people view what is theirs (how ever great or small) as theirs and consider their personal property an important safeguard for their family. They rely on government to protect their rights and property but recognize that government can also be a threat to those rights and property. History and experience tells them that if government is allowed to take from one's neighbor today, one's own might be at risk tomorrow. The view of government as a threat against which people need and want protection, while contrary to Robeyns's philosophy, is very much part of the American heritage and a pillar supporting the American Dream.

The real irony, almost too painful me to discuss, is that while the principal alleged adverse impact of inequality of wealth is the undermining of social cohesion, the principal exhortation in the book is to become activists. Activists for what? To undermine social cohesion by convincing the currently complacent citizenry that they are victims.

"The first and perhaps most important action limitarianism requires is one that we've already touched on: to dismantle neoliberal ideology, because it is at the heart of the problems we are facing. ...As long as neoliberalism is our dominant ideology, fighting its consequences will be insufficient. We must therefore attack the root cause and replace neoliberalism with something more humane... ." *Id.*, pp. 215-216.

"We must share this critique with everyone." *Id.*, p.217.

"I have dedicated this book to all activists who are fighting against injustice. ...[N]ot only to those who are on the barricades, but also to those writing pieces for newspapers, setting up organizations, and trying in other ways to mobilize people and power for the good." *Id.*, p.235.

She bases this call to activism on the assertion that the regular people are ignorant of the facts and fail to see their self-interests accurately.

"To what extent are ordinary people aware of today's immense economic inequality? Do they know that this inequality is not 'natural,' by any means? Do they know that the dominant classes have quietly established a set of global economic rules that favor their own interests, that they have influenced national decisions on taxes and spending, and that ... they have largely sought to improve their own financial position? ...I'd venture that many people have no idea how deep the problem goes. Such ignorance applies to everyone— the rich, the poor, and the middle classes."

Id., p.204.

"Why does this matter? Well, if people perceive or believe that inequalities are high, they might well make stronger demands for redistribution. If, as is the case, they are mistaken in believing that inequalities are smaller than they really are, their demands for redistribution will be more timid." *Id.*, p.206.

Remedies

Robeyns claims that the disrepute of Communism is used (unfairly) to discredit limitarianism.

She acknowledges the widespread rejection of Communism, describing it as follows:

> "[T]he dominant view has been that the communist experiment failed. Some citizens had spent years trying to escape these countries, but by that point the majority had decided they had had enough of living in repressive regimes while across the border people were living much better lives. ...There was severe political repression that infiltrated all levels of society; you could not be sure that your aunt or friend wasn't a spy for the state. In several countries, the state made important personal decisions for its citizens, such as who could study and what subject."

Id., p 207.

Yet, she identifies the reason the rejection as the dislike of "despotic central planning of the economy by the government, a feature to which she herself objects. Thus, she argues that since limitarianism does not necessarily require central planning, the attack based upon characterizing it as similar to Communism is a devious ploy to misled the masses. Indeed,

> "...the suggestion that limitarianism is akin to communism is also very sad, perhaps even maddening, since it indicates that, all too often, the opponents of progressive ideas are not really interested in having a genuine discussion about these proposals. Instead, they want to caricature them in a way that they know will put many people off the discussion entirely."

Id., p.208.

She totally disrards the issue of the loss of freedoms. That omission is extraordinarily telling as she proceeds to set forth te necessary first six steps in the implementation of limitarianism:

- Change how people think. "[D]ismantle neoliberal ideology... ." *Id.*, pp. 215-216.
- Alter where and how the people live.
  "The second thing limitarianism requires is that we reduce class segregation. We must do so because it will directly help to restore and nurture democracy, in particular democratic citizenship. ...Alas, relying on voluntary action will not do the trick. If class desegregation is made voluntary, then we can expect that many very rich and privileged people will not join in." *Id.*, pp.217-8.
- Revise our economic institutions. "The third action limitarianism requires is for us to establish a balance of economic power." *Id.*, p.219.
- Strengthen government revenue raising. *Id.*, p.221.
- Confiscate "dirty" money and pay reparations. *Id.*, p.222.

- Stop the transfer of wealth within families. "[T]he most urgent of all... ." *Id.*, p.226.

That is for starters.

Whose happiness is Robeyns seeking to promote?

Her own and of those who share her political values. It makes me want to cry.

Probably my greatest divergence in views is with respect to the societal consequences of having significant assets in the hands of governments rather than of private individuals. Robeyns clearly, longingly perceives that prospect as the benefit propelling her policy recommendations.

"We need limitarianism because there is a clear case to be made against extreme wealth concentration. But we also need limitarianism because there is so much good that money above the riches line could do, if only it were used for addressing collective problems." *Id.*, p.117.

"The bottom line is simply this: there is so much good our governments could do with the excess money of the super-rich. And taking it from them would probably not affect their welfare at all—not in any meaningful sense. If there is a slight drop in the luxury of their lifestyles, it would be massively outweighed by the gains to others, and the gains to the common good." *Id.*, p.159.

I, in contrast, see it as a great uncertainty. Undoubtedly, very good and desirable things could conceivably be realized, but what is most likely to happen?

There are two different types of concerns about transferring assets to government. The first is government inefficiency, waste and corruption. The problem is the inherent lack of accountability compared to the private sector. There exists everywhere temptations inviting laziness, inattention and corruption. There will everywhere incompetence, misjudgements, errors and accidents; but, the private sector has an impersonal, ruthless and tireless overseer—competition—that the public sector lacks. The second is that decisions as to the use of the assets will be made through the political process run by politicians. Experience demonstrates how treacherous reliance on politicians is likely to be. I simply do not think it accurate to claim that political spending decisions reflect the will of the people or tend to promote the general well being.

Robeyns is critical of private philanthropy where there is significant inequality because it is "undemocratic." I, however, am severely disappointed in the political process' handling of budgeting and spending.

One should recognize that governments have played a significant role in increasing inequality over the last 50 years. Governments own more than $100 trillion of assets consisting of land, infrastructure and natural resources, in addition to financial assets. That wealth can be attributed to their citizens per capita—roughly $12,000 per person. However, over the last 50 years, public debt has soared, largely spent on current consumption rather than invested in public assets, thus reducing public net worth.

In effect, governments borrowed against public assets, giving the proceeds to only some of their citizens who then spent it. The result is that in much of the world, including the U.S. And the U.K., the public net worth is now negative. There is per capita public debt rather than public wealth.

"The total public sector assets in the [38] countries covered are worth $103 trillion. … These assets consist of public infrastructure such as bridges and roads, financial assets such as bank deposits, as well as natural resource reserves in the ground. Total liabilities stand at $93 trillion. This comprises some $44 trillion of general government debt, but also includes $22 trillion of current pension obligations and the debt of state-owned enterprises. Net worth—assets minus liabilities—comes to $10 trillion … ."

Jason Harris, Abdelhak Senhadji, "A Global Picture of Public Wealth," *IMF Blog*, June 18, 2019.

"In advanced economies, fiscal deficits soared as countries saw revenues collapse due to the recession and put in place sweeping fiscal measures as COVID-19 spread. Public debt rose 19 percentage points of GDP, in 2020, an increase like that seen during the global financial crisis, over two years: 2008 and 2009." Vitor Gaspar, Paulo Medas, Roberto Perrelli, "Global Debt Reaches a Record $226 Trillion," *IMF Blog*, December 15, 2021.

"Global debt has hit a record $300 trillion, or 349% leverage on gross domestic product. This translates to $37,500 of average debt for each person in the world versus GDP per capita of just $12,000. Government debt-to-GDP leverage grew aggressively, by 76%, to a total of 102%, from 2007 to 2022." Terry Chan, "Global Debt Leverage: Is a Great Reset Coming? Rising rates and slowing economies mean the world's high leverage poses a crisis risk," *S&P Global Ratings*, January 13, 2023.

The relationship between income broadly defined (including unrealized appreciation) and wealth is current consumption. Thus, it is safe to bet that the result of a significant transfer of wealth from the super rich to the bottom half, directly or through governments as intermediaries, would quickly result in the reduction in total wealth and an increase in current consumption. Remember that the total wealth of the households with at least $500 million is around $20 trillion. Divided among roughly 3 billion households in the world, that amount would provide about $6,700 per household, and that would be a one-time payment. How much of that do you think would be saved and invested? And, what would be the impact of the sudden increase in consumer demand? Well, we have just been experiencing a trial run. The result is inflation.

The fact is that inequality assists the creation of wealth and economic growth.

Robeyns is correct that property, wealth and markets depend upon, are created by, organized society and government. Thus, each person's rights are defined by and subject to the rules of that society and government. "Limitarianism rests on the fundamental philosophical insight that markets and property are social institutions. ...[I]n the world as it is, there is no property, and there are no markets, outside the social context... ." *Id.*, p.118.

Robeyns seems to like island hypotheticals. It is probably correct that no one would become super rich stranded on an island, but hierarchies based on individual strengths would probably arise. *See, e.g.*, the play *The Admirable Crichton* by James Matthew Barrie (1902). "[P]ut them on a desert island. They still have all the same talents and personal traits as before. How rich could they become? Not very rich, obviously. ...[W]ithout collective institutions, public goods, basic infrastructure, and collaboration with other people, it would be impossible for anyone to become rich—in other words, that we all rely on the social contract." *Id.*, pp.135, 137.

At the same time, the authority of that government and the society to impose burdens on or require sacrifices from its citizens is constrained by those rules. The balance between the individual's rights to pursue his own self interest and the individual's obligations to society will be a defining feature of that society.

CHAPTER 7

Books Still Unwritten

I realize that looking at my writings from a distance one could easily conclude that I do not consider racism, global warming or inequality to be problems. That would be incorrect. However, I do recognize that my understanding of the nature of those problems my views of possible solutions differ from the accepted elite liberal consensus.

I have pretty much said everything I have to say about climate change, but there are still books I wanted to write about racism and inequality. I lack the strength to do the appropriate research and analysis. So, those books remain unwritten. Here, based on my reading and writing to date, however, is a summary of what I think those books would say.

I.

Darwinism and Race

I have expressed the opinion that Social Darwinism and eugenics need to be discussed on the scientific merits, not just condemned on moral grounds.

"[T]he societal response following the exposure of the Nazi atrocities was to ban the discussion of these subjects and to condemn the proponents. ...[That] may have been the most appropriate approach at the time, but we may (perhaps) have reached a sufficient distance to permit an analysis on the merits. By that I mean ... assess the scientific merits of the theories and arguments... ." *Supra*, pp.114-5

The points of such an analysis would probably be, more or less, the following:

1. To the extent one attempts to define race genetically, one must rely on the existence of clusters of overlapping traits. There are no definitive or dispositive markers.

"Once out of Africa, these populations remained isolated from one another —separated by mountains, oceans, or great distances. As a result of living and reproducing in unique environments for tens of thousands of years, each group's gene pool evolved in response to the unique selection pressures of its environment. The legacy of these genetic differences is still visible and measurable today. Although each of us is genetically unique (barring identical twins), each of us also belongs to clusters of similar genomes whose similarity stems from the major out-of-Africa migrations that occurred tens of thousands of years ago. These clusters are not sharply separated from one another. They overlap a great deal, and therefore the boundaries between them are blurry."

Coleman Hughes, The End of Race Politics: Arguments for a Colorblind America (2024), pp.4-5.

2. All genetic traits occur following normal distributions represented by Bell curves.

"Most people, of course, are in the middle of the range, displaying mixtures of reciprocity, pure generosity, and greed. Why do people range across such a wide spectrum? Perhaps all of us are capable of being saints or sinners, depending on the temptations and threats at hand. Perhaps we are predisposed to being nastier or nicer by our genes. "

Steven Pinker, *The Blank Slate: The Modern Denial of Human Nature* (2002, 2016), p.260.

3. As a result, variations in the means or averages between groups are irrelevant to the assessment or prospects of individuals in either group. There will always be some members of either group that will be ranked higher than many members of the other group, and some in each group that will be ranked lower than many in the other.

"If various characteristics are to a non-trivial extent determined by genetics (say, height, body type or athletic ability, or, more relevant here, intelligence, temperament, self-discipline or ambition), then not only will individuals differ to varying degrees, but groups of people with genetic similarities greater than average (families, stable communities, isolated populations, races, tight knit religious groups) will vary statistically from one another. For example, the average heights, IQs, motivation, dedication, focus, discipline (if they could be quantified and averaged) will vary from group to group. Importantly, however, nothing much can be said about any particular individual. He or she may have had a greater or lesser probability *ex ante* of being smarter or taller than someone else, but after-the-fact, they either are or are not." *Politics*, History and Ideology, pp.42-3.

4. Genetic diversity is highly beneficial; excessive inbreeding is seriously detrimental.

"The new version of Darwin and Spencer's great theory, which includes both competitive and cooperative evolution (phylogenetic and ontogenetic learning), tells us that for fundamental reasons there is **strength in diversity**. This on the surface sounds very different than the notion of survival of the fittest, but we will see how these statements are really two sides of the same coin."

Bobby Azarian, *The Romance of Reality: How the Universe Organizes Itself to Create Life, Consciousness, and Cosmic Complexity* (2024), p.124.

See also, James Woodford, "Modern rose hybrids have a worrying lack of genetic diversity: Intensive breeding since the 19th century has created thousands of varieties of rose, but a reduction in genetic diversity could leave them vulnerable to diseases and climate change," *New Scientist*, 25 April 2024.

5. Individual performance is only partially determined by genetics.

"'The effects of differences in genes on differences in minds can be measured, and the same rough estimate—substantially greater than zero, but substantially less than 100 percent—pops out of the data no matter what measuring stick is used.' *Id.*, p.47. 'A conventional summary is that **about half of the variation in intelligence, personality, and life outcomes is heritable**—a correlate or an indirect product of the genes. ...' *Id.*, p.374 (emphasis added)."

Politics, History and Ideology, p.37, citing Steven Pinker, *The Blank Slate*.

6. Finally, the genetic future of the species will be safe, The more able will not be outcompeted by the less able for resources and, thus, disappear—they will survive, even if increasingly outnumbered.

"It is entirely possible in a modern, industrialized nation for the less able to out-reproduce the more able, especially if the survival rates are not too disparate—a reversal of the model of Darwinian evolution. [Not that I am concerned about the genetic future of the species from this phenomenon (unlike things like increasing pollution or toxins causing more frequent mutations). The more able will not be outcompeted by the less able for resources and, thus, disappear. They will survive, even if increasingly outnumbered. These stronger genetic makeups will still be here, ready to resurge following the next apocalypse, just as in *The Walking Dead*. And, as in that TV series, some of the capable will be good and some will be evil.]"

Politics, History and Ideology, p.53.

These propositions constitute a strong rebuttal of eugenics .

II.

Racism without Race

I know that there are people who base judgments on race alone, but I think the significance of those people diminished dramatically during the twentieth century. I suggest that since at least the 1960s, racism has been less and less about race and more about behavior, lifestyle and cultural characteristics. Indeed, even Presidents Lincoln and Teddy Roosevelt apparently found education, courage and deportment to outweigh race.

"[Fredrick] Douglass understood that Lincoln's ideas about Black people changed over the course of the war. The president had been deeply moved by the valor of the Black men who'd helped save the Union and had been influenced by Black men such as Douglass, whom he held in high esteem. ....In his final speech before his assassination, Lincoln expressed an openness to enfranchising a limited number of Black men—particularly educated men and those who'd fought in the war."

Nikole Hannah-Jones, The New York Times Magazine, Caitlin Roper, Ilena Silverman, and Jake Silverstein, *The 1619 Project: A New Origin Story* (2021), p.26.

"Principles of fair play told Roosevelt that nothing should inhibit the individuals in any group who have the ability to achieve great success. The extraordinary achievements of black men such as Washington were dramatic proof of this to Roosevelt. But at the same time, Roosevelt believed that, collectively, no one should or reasonably could deny the obvious racial superiority of whites over all others."

Douglas A. Blackmon, *Slavery by Another Name: The Re-Enslavement of Black Americans from the Civil War to World War II* (2008), p.163.

In my years of young adulthood, I perceived danger not from race but from dress and group behavior. The cultivated appearance of a tough, violent persona was the warning. It is hard for me to think this prejudice unacceptable. It was certainly rational and justified by what we observed in the streets and on the subways of New York City in the 1970s. Was it fair? That is hard to answer. However, one's dress and manner have traditionally been considered displays of respect or disrespect. People are free to choose to rebel or to refuse to conform, but what is obligation of others to minimize the consequences of one's choice?

The level of crime and drug trafficking in the inner cities by 1970 was of major concern. The "story" today is that the Republicans made it a political issue. Of course they did play to it, but drug-related crime was a political issue, a serious one, because drug-related crime was a serious societal issue and concern both in the suburbs and in the inner cities. It is fair to criticize the government efforts to address the problem, but it is ridiculous to claim today that the wrong was the political use of the issue rather than the destructive behavior that was occurring.

The increased militancy of the Black communities in 2013 onward and the rather sharp criticisms leveled by both Blacks and whites against the establishment heightened emotions and placed race as a central factor in the national dialogue. *See supra.,* pp. Nonetheless, the emerging national divide was not based on race, but on political philosophies. Well, perhaps not so much political philosophies as lifestyle and asserted values, increasingly polarized by group social pressures and social media. A significant portion of the population has been labeled as inferior, as less intelligent, less enlightened, less human, as "deplorables." Very reminiscent of the expressions of Jim Crow sentiments.

Racism without race. And, a view greatly exasperated, and used, by Donald Trump.

It is graduation season and commencement ceremonies are occurring across the country.

President Biden delivered a commencement speech to the graduating class at Moorhead University. It was filled with overly indulgent self promotion (an astonishingly frequent use of "I" for a commencement speech).

But, then he said:

> "You all know and demonstrate what it really means to be a man. Being a man is about the strength of **respect and dignity**. It's about showing up because it's too late if you have to ask. It's about **giving hate no safe harbor** and leaving no one behind and **defending freedoms**. It's about standing up to the abuse of power, whether physical, economic, or psychological. It's about knowing faith without works is dead."

President Biden's Morehouse College Commencement Address, May 19, 2024 (emphasis added).

Quite right. If he meant it.

But, the immediately preceding sentences were:

> "[T]his is what we're up against: extremist forces aligned against the meaning and message of Morehouse. And they peddle a fiction, a caricature what being a man is about—tough talk, abusing power, bigotry. Their idea of being a man is toxic. I ran into them all the time when I was younger. They got—all right, I don't want to get started. (Laughter.)"

Respect and dignity? No, denunciation, demonization and distain.

The self-congratulatory hypocrisy of the self-anointed morally superior class.

For a sharp contrast, consider this account of the contemporaneous words of the retiring President of Notre Dame addressing that graduating class:

> "Father John Jenkins, the [Notre Dame] university president for the past 19 years, is stepping down this summer. On Sunday he apologized to the graduating class that they had him rather than Taylor Swift or another exciting celebrity as their commencement speaker. Then he turned serious and urged them to pursue the values of toleration and openness to others and to resist the temptation to demonize others: **'The invitation to vilify an opponent is so seductive, perhaps because it can seem like a confirmation of our own virtue. If we speak only to those with whom we agree, our contempt for the evil opposition can seem like a sign of our own moral superiority.'"**

Gerard Baker, "Higher Ed Has a Progressive Disease. Can It Be Reversed?" *WSJ.com*, May 20, 2024 (emphasis added).

As Bill Maher recently remarked: "Today, 94% of adults are cool with interracial marriage; it's interparty marriage that's a deal breaker. In 1960, only 5% of Americans had a negative reaction to the idea of marrying someone from a different political party; now it's 38%." "Red and Blue America Can't Just Go Their Separate Ways," *WSJ.com*, May 17, 2024.

A fine state of affairs.

III.

Extreme Wealth

I have written about the inevitability of inequality and the benefits therefrom. *Politics, History and Ideology*, pp.115-201 However, we have levels of wealth held by a small percentage of people that are neither inevitable nor socially beneficial. How much is too much? One could argue that anything more than a billion dollars of assets for a single family unit is more than can be justified. I think that in today's environment, we should categorize as extreme wealth family holdings of more than 10 billion dollars.

So, if we conclude that no strong case can be made in support of extreme wealth, can we also conclude that such wealth is injurious to society? I am skeptical of many of the common arguments, like too much political influence and social unrest. I think that they are overblown and factually incorrect. However, I think that the problem is that these extremely wealthy individuals have control over a percentage of national and global investment funds that is inconsistent with a pluralistic market economy. These few individuals decide the allocation of too much of the total capital investment. The solution for this problem is not a redistribution of wealth from the top .001% to the bottom half. Such a change would increase current consumption and reduce capital investment because the recipients would spend the funds rather than invest them, most likely hampering economic growth. So, the preferable redistribution would be within the top quintile. That would support capital investment while broadening substantially the number of people making investment decisions.

Since the sources of most of extreme wealth will be economic rents, redistribution after the fact, even if fully anticipated, should not distort the allocation of productive resources while still allowing market pricing to allocate consumption. This was the rationale of Henry George's proposal to tax away essentially all the gains in the market values of land. *Progress and Poverty* (1879).

It is superficially easy to imagine a tax on excess wealth, but it is difficult to imagine how those revenues could be utilized to promote greater dispersion of investment decision making. Having government invest most of the revenues, say in infrastructure, would further increase, not decrease consolidation of decision-making. The distribution per capita or to the needy would reduce invested capital.

We can put some rough numbers on the features of interest. The total global net non-financial assets in 2023 had a value of about $510 trillion, a rather dramatic increase from 2000.

"The real economy balance sheet has $520 trillion in real assets, such as machinery and equipment, infrastructure, buildings, natural resources, and intellectual property, or IP. These are mirrored on the liability side as net worth."

...

"At the global level, real assets constitute net worth, while aggregate financial assets and liabilities net to zero... ."

...

"The global balance sheet and net worth more than tripled between 2000 and 2020. net worth grew from $160 trillion to $510 trillion."

Lola Woetzel, Jan Mischke, Anu Madgavkar, Eckart Windhagen, Sven Smit, Michael Birshan, Szabolcs Kemeny, and Rebecca J. Anderson, "The rise of the global balance sheet: How productively are we using our wealth?," *McKinsey & Company*, 2024.

Of that total, about half is residential real estate. Only about 20%, or $100 trillion, represents productive capital assets.

"The value of residential real estate including land amounted to 46 percent of global net worth in 2020, with corporate and government buildings and the land associated with them accounting for an additional 23 percent. Other fixed assets like infrastructure, industrial structures, machinery and equipment, intangibles, and mineral reserves—the types of assets that typically drive economic growth—made up only one-fifth of real assets or net worth, ranging from 15 percent in the United Kingdom and France to 39 percent in Japan... ." *Id.*

There are about 2,700 households (individuals or families) with assets worth a billion dollars or more (the top being around $180 billion). Those billionaires hold assets worth $14.2 trillion.

"There are now more billionaires than ever: 2,781 in all, 141 more than last year and 26 more than the record set in 2021. They're richer than ever, worth $14.2 trillion in aggregate, up by $2 trillion from 2023 and $1.1 trillion above the previous record, also set in 2021." *Forbes Billionaires 2024*, "The Richest People In The World".

Of that group, some 200 households with more than $10 billion each hold assets totaling about $7 trillion. Thus, 200 households control almost 7% of the world's capital investment, and fewer than 3,000 households control almost 14%. That is a rather high level of concentration of control. Other measures give comparable results.

"The scale of inequality between the income quintiles grows at the top. The top 20% group has over four times as much wealth as the fourth 20%, which has close to double the wealth of the third 20%. The second 20% has around 1.3 times as much wealth as the bottom 20%. [T]he top 1% has more than half the wealth of the rest of the top 20% collectively.

"The top 1% has more in stocks and mutual funds as the rest of the top 20% combined.... . The differences in scale continue down the income quintiles. The top 20% has more than 10 times as much wealth in stocks/mutual funds as the next 20%. The fourth 20% has three times as much wealth in stocks/mutual funds as the middle income quintile. Those in the second and bottom 20% have similar wealth in stocks and mutual funds... ."

[The charts show that the top 20% hold $30 trillion in stocks and mutual funds, while everyone else holds about $4.5 trillion.. The top 1% holds over $15 trillion.]

USAFacts Team, "How this chart explains Americans' wealth across income levels: The top 1% of households in America represent 26% of total US wealth," *USAFacts.org*, March 28, 2023.

Most of the increase in net worth since 2000 came from increases in asset valuations, especially in real estate, caused largely by falling interest rates, not from an increase in assets, such as through new capital investment.

"Net worth has tripled since 2000, but the increase mainly reflects valuation gains in real assets, especially real estate, rather than investment in productive assets that drive our economies."

...

"Of the net worth gains tied to real estate at the global level, some 55 percent derived from higher land prices, while 24 percent was attributable to higher construction costs. The remaining 21 percent was a result of net investment—that is, construction of new homes or improvements to existing ones less wear and tear."

McKinsey & Company.

Most governments now have negative net worth, with debt exceeding asset value. McKinsey concludes that increased global investment is a priority need.

> "Real assets are critical to the global economy. Returns on those assets account for about one-quarter of GDP directly. Growth in real assets also complements labor in driving productivity, which in turn drives economic growth. ...[R]edirecting capital to more productive and sustainable uses seems to be the economic imperative of our time, not only to support growth and the environment but also to protect our wealth and financial systems."

Id.

So, what about taxes?

I have previously set out a proposal for the revision of the U.S. System which would both broaden the tax base and increase the effective income tax collected from the highest income individuals. I do not think, however, that these reforms would have much effect on inequality or extreme wealth. The primary reason is that extreme wealth generally arises from ownership of the results of entrepreneurial activities and appreciation in asset values that are not realized income so are not taxed as income until sold. Thus, for example, Sweden, despite high income tax rates, has experienced a significant wealth inequality and has a large number of billionaires.

"Sweden has a global reputation for championing high taxes and social equality, but it has become a European hotspot for the super rich."

...

"Recent research from Örebro University concluded that the media image of Swedish billionaires is predominantly positive ... . 'As long as the super-rich are seen to embody the ideals of the neoliberal era, such as hard work, taking risks, and an entrepreneurial attitude, the inequality behind this is not questioned,' says media researcher Axel Vikström."

Maddy Savage, "The rise of Sweden's super rich," *BBC News, Stockholm,* 6 May 2024.

Proposals to change the system to tax unrealized appreciation in assets threaten to undermine economic growth and entrepreneurial success by forcing the sales of assets to pay the taxes. And, it would be only fair to also recognize unrealized losses. The result would be complicated and costly. One possible approach would be to make the borrowing of money secured by assets an income realization event, comparable to a sale of an interest in the assets. At least, the taxpayer would be receiving money with which to pay the tax.

The other approach to reducing wealth through taxation is to change the estate tax system. Progressive rates is one possibility. Say, amounts in an estate greater than $100 million could be taxed at 50%, amounts greater than $500 at 70%. Another approach would be to eliminate the stepped up basis in assets at death. Then, the appreciation would get taxed as income at some point, when realized. One consequence would be that if the estate sold appreciated assets to pay estate taxes, income tax tax would be due on the realized gain. Thus, for example, the sale of assets with a gain of $100 million would be subject to the capital gains tax, say 20%, and the remainder, $80 million, would be subject to the estate tax, say 40%, for a combined tax rate of 52%.

What about the proposed "wealth tax"?

It is like the property tax. A key source of controversy would be valuation. Even for marketable securities, issues would arise with respect to large holdings (Would a hypothetical sale be expected to depress the price and by how much? Could there be a control premium?). And, such a tax would encourage tax-avoidance activities. France has a wealth tax. It is successfully avoided by the wealthy through holding financial assets outside of France and buying property with large mortgages. The banks appear to be the main beneficiaries of the tax. The mortgage rates are reasonable enough, but the. banks require life insurance from captive insurance companies at rates about three times the market.

Anyway, for purposes of this discussion, the most significant fact is that a wealth tax of 1% to 3% simply would not materially reduce extreme wealth.

CHAPTER 8

Dreams ...

**"I had hopes and dreams
but now I have bills and taxes."**

The above quotation popped up on my Facebook feed. I have no attribution, but then it is not very original nor particularly profound. However, it is suggestive of the nature of the transition from childhood to adulthood. Seeing it started me thinking.

Hopes and Dreams

As often the case with cliches, we repeat them or endorse them without thinking about their actual meaning. Of course, young people have dreams. Yet, try as I might, I cannot actually recall having any myself. Oh, I had lots of fantasies, Walter Mitty style, and I felt ambition, a desire to compete and win. But, not dreams. No vision of the life to which I aspired, of what would make me happy and satisfied.

I remember my worst job interview. I was beginning my second year of law school. The young partner at a prestigious law firm leaned back with a smile and asked: "So, how do you see yourself five years from now?" He was clearly relishing how clever he was. I was silent, slowly panicking. I had no answer of my own. I had no idea what answer he expected or would like. He got me.

Thinking back on it, I realize that the question was stupid. I was 23, looking to be a summer associate at a top-tier law firm to see what it was like. I knew nothing about law firms and only a little about the practice of law. I had no image or vision or, even, expectation of myself 5 years in the future. Moreover, as I now appreciate, if I became a law firm associate upon graduation, then in 5 years from that interview, I would either be a hard working mid-level associate or out looking for another job.

My expectations were that a summer at a law firm would tell whether I could handle being an associate and give me a hint of whether I could see myself as a partner, if things went well over the following seven or so years. Then, I might be able to see myself 5 years into that future. The question makes little sense for me today, obviously; but, I am not sure that there was ever a point where 5 years was a meaningful time horizon.

If we dial back the concept of dreams to things less grand, I did have some. I longed to learn to paint. I saw myself seated at an easel in various scenic parts of the world seeking to capture glimpses of beauty with oils on canvas. As a poor substitute more compatible with travel companions, I tried photography. I got some impressive results among masses of pretty typical travel shots.

I bought an easel, dozens of tubes of oil paints, brushes and canvases of all sizes. But, I hesitated, continuously, for years. I told myself that I did not have the time, but I think I knew somewhere inside that I did not have the talent and did not want to have to face it. After I retired and settled in Cambridge, I attempted to learn. It was consuming, but I quickly realized that I could not use an easel. My back, neck and arms lacked the strength. I could only manage by hunching over a canvas laid flat on a table. Of course, my weakness relentlessly continued to increase until I could simply not longer continue.

Another fantasy that emerged during the three years I worked in London was that I would open an art gallery to exhibit the paintings I would buy as I traveled to auctions around the world. During those years, I became a regular visitor at the viewings at the London auction houses. I generally bid online, but I selected the works through in person visits. I recognized that photos were often deceptive. I found that I could promptly identify the paintings of potential interest though a quick look through the galleries. A second, close inspection confirmed or terminated my interest. Well, that dream was not to be realized either. However, I have been indulging myself. I have been buying paintings at auction. Many. I have compromised on in person viewing and accepted the risks of relying of photographs and written descriptions. So, I have made several mistakes. I limit the exposure by restricting my maximum bids severely. It is fascinating and exciting. I love inspecting my purchases. I am running out of space, since I want them all accessible to sight from my wheelchair. But, I am probably running out of time anyway.

I read that it is hope that keeps people alive. I have probably even expressed that sentiment myself. But, hope for what, I wonder.

Christopher Reeve was apparently motivated by hope—hope for a cure through stem cell therapy, if it could be approved and available in time. He was a quadriplegic as the result of a fall from a horse while jumping. An effective treatment was conceivable (although, not realized).

"When we have hope, we discover powers within ourselves we may have never known—the power to make sacrifices, to endure, to heal, and to love. Once we choose hope, everything is possible." Christopher Reeve, *Nothing Is Impossible: Reflections on a New Life* (2002), p.177.

But, ALS is different. There is no potential treatment that has been identified, only experimental research.

"Hopes and dreams"? They would be nice, I guess.

Maybe.

Acceptance

Steve Gleason (of Team Gleason) recounts his rather frantic years, criss-crossing the country in search for a cure, before he "accepted" his fate. Steve Gleason, Jeff Duncan, *A Life Impossible: Living with ALS: Finding Peace and Wisdom Within a Fragile Existence* (2024). He notes:"I was reminded of a story a doctor told me about a family where the dad was diagnosed with ALS, and the children said that he spent four years chasing his tail trying to find a cure, but he never woke up to watch the sun rise. So, what would I do with the time I had left? I planned to fully live—and watch the sun rise." *Id.*, p.131. Yet, later: "We knew these alternative treatments were long shots, but what other choice did we really have? If we hadn't gone through with these therapies, we would have stayed up at night, torturing ourselves with questions like 'What if we'd done the stem-cell therapy and it worked?' ... Better to regret something you did than something you didn't do." *Id*, p.166.

It is a difficult choice.

Gleason lives an unusual life. He is surrounded by friends able and willing to assist, many of whom are young, strong and athletic, and finds generous funding. He, with his crew, has done some amazing things, beyond the wildest imagination of those of us with ALS. Yet, I cannot suppress the image of the king too obese to walk, and who can barely lift his arms, being carried in his litter by four men to the feast where he is fed by attendants. What made me uncomfortable is Gleason's apparent failure to recognize how unusual and special his situation is. When writing about my (first) decade with ALS, I was continuously concerned about not minimizing difficulties that I, unlike many others, could manage only because of my financial resources. I thought about what I could say that might be relevant and helpful to the large number of sufferers and families in different situations.

In, I think, 2019, a good friend sent me an article about Peter Scott-Morgan, suggesting she saw some similarities. I have been unable to find what she sent, but my recollection is that it was similar in tone to his book, *Peter 2.0* (2021), which I just discovered.

"We've got two years before statistically I should be dead. That means we've got two years to rewrite the future. And change the world.

"There'll be battles all the way, and then the ultimate life-or-death show-down. Either we'll win, in which case everything will change, or we'll very conspicuously fail. Which isn't going to happen. There can be no middle ground.

"MND expects me to die. I refuse.

"I also refuse merely to 'stay alive' in a form of living death.

"Also—a complete revelation to me as the thought distilled and suddenly became recognisable – I refuse too to leave everyone else behind, traumatised by their two-year death sentence, scared to die, terrified to live. We'll gather an army. We'll build a movement. This is rebellion!"

He laid out a proactive plan to use technology and surgical procedures to preempt the unpleasant consequences of the disease's progression. A would be superman. In fact, at the time, I was offended and annoyed by the article, through no fault of my friend. I think it was what I perceived as his arrogance, even smugness, that upset me.

Recently, some five years later, I recalled my earlier reaction and decided to see what had happened to Peter. I discovered that he had died in 2022, almost 6 years after his diagnosis. I also realized that I had been unfair in my judgment. Peter had an educational and work background that shaped his response. He turned to what he knew. And, he saw an opportunity to pursue and promote some of his ideas publicly. He succeeded in getting the publicity, if not in beating the disease.

"An English scientist known as the world's first human cyborg has died at 64.

"Dr. Peter Scott-Morgan made headlines in 2020 as the subject of the documentary 'Peter: The Human Cyborg.' The film followed the groundbreaking scientist's journey as he refused to accept his terminal diagnosis and worked to become fully robotic to extend his life after he was diagnosed with motor neuron disease... .

"Scott-Morgan, who had a Ph.D. in robotics, developed an incredibly lifelike avatar to smile and express his emotions as his face muscles failed, had a voice box fitted with his own recorded speech, used eye-tracking technology to operate computers and used a wheelchair that allowed him to stand and lie flat."

Adriana Diaz, "Dr. Peter Scott-Morgan, 'world's first human cyborg,' dead at 64," *New York Post*, June 15, 2022.

"Few people could be better placed than this 62-year-old to battle the effects of this neurological condition and win. He is a scientist with an interest in artificial intelligence (AI), and his PhD from Imperial College London was the first ever granted by a robotics faculty in Britain. ...While he might not have been able to articulate the finer details of his plan in that moment, every synapse in his brain was firing. 'I refuse simply to stay alive,' he writes, 'I choose to THRIVE!' It was simplistic, he says, almost adolescent obstinacy."

Michael Segalov, "'I choose to thrive': the man fighting motor neurone disease with cyborg technology," *The Guardian*, 16 August 2022.

I viewed the diagnosis of ALS differently than what is generally reflected in the public commentary. A few years ago, it seemed to me that the ALS Association in the States formulated its campaign in terms of a fight. But, not a collective fight against the disease. Each victim was to stand up to ALS—ALS will not beat me. A personal battle. The emphasis has changed, I think. Now, research to find a cure to prevent its future occurrence and efforts to improve the quality of life for current sufferers. ("Let's see more care. Let's see a cure. Let's See It End. Together, let's ensure that everyone, everywhere, can access the care they need." May 2024.) A very sensible approach—the tacit recognition that a cure that would enable current sufferers to recover, reversing the decline, is highly improbable.

I see ALS as a circumstance with which I am confronted, not as an enemy. For me, the question was what is the best life I can live given the circumstances.

I think my view is quite elegantly captured by the frequently quoted prayer attributed to Reinhold Niebuhr:

> God, grant me the serenity to accept
> the things I cannot change,
> the courage to change the things I can,
> and the wisdom to know the difference.

I choose acceptance almost from the beginning. Of course, I was already 67 years old. Spending what might have been my last two years trying to find a miracle that would grant me a relatively few more seemed foolish, a bad gamble, especially because I had a few things I needed to do.

My mother's father, after my grandmother died, calmly organized his affairs, visited and checked on all of his grandchildren, then passed away. My father's father, in contrast, died from a sudden, unexpected heart attack. The results were chaotic. He had recently bought an annuity. I opened the envelope containing the first annuity check dated two days after he died. I do not mean to suggest that he had not planned responsibly—my grandmother lived comfortably for many more years—but, I was keenly aware of the impact of death on others. Forty years later, minimizing the adverse impact of my death on my family was my primary concern.

If I had suffered this development in my mid-30s (or, if it had been a disease with real treatment options), my response could have been quite different. Two more years, while a greater percentage of the life one had lived, may seem trivial to one expecting an additional 40-50 years, but significant to someone was anticipating only another 10 years.

Regrets

Reading comments about end of life experiences, I see frequent references to regrets. *See, e.g.*, Philippa Kelly, "'My life will be short. So on the days I can, I really live': 30 dying people explain what really matters," *The Guardian*, 27 January 2024; Grace Bluerock, "The 9 Most Common Regrets People Have At The End Of Life," *mindbody-green.com*, July 07, 2023. It strikes me as odd. I have many memories that leave me embarrassed, some that leave me puzzled, but none that leave me feeling regret. I can understand regretting actions taken, or not taken, that have adverse consequences for my life now, like smoking too much or saving too little, but not having partied more or not having been more adventurous (or promiscuous) seem kind of irrelevant to my life now. I guess memories are a source of pleasure (or pain), but I have enough myself and I cannot say for others.

Curiosity

In examining myself, I think that what keeps me alive is not hope, but curiosity. I am interested in things, very interested in some, mildly so in many others. And, my interests change. But, in all events, it is the compulsion to learn more, to see what happens next, that keeps me going. I don't want to miss anything.

"'Sir Ector has given me a glass of canary,' said the Wart, 'and sent me to see if you can't cheer me up.' 'Sir Ector,' said Merlyn, 'is a wise man.'

"'Well,' said the Wart, 'what about it?'

"'The best thing for being sad,' replied Merlyn, beginning to puff and blow, 'is to learn something. That is the only thing that never fails. You may grow old and trembling in your anatomies, you may lie awake at night listening to the disorder of your veins, you may miss your only love, you may see the world about you devastated by evil lunatics, or know your honour trampled in the sewers of baser minds. There is only one thing for it then—to learn. Learn why the world wags and what wags it. That is the only thing which the mind can never exhaust, never alienate, never be tortured by, never fear or distrust, and never dream of regretting.'

...

"'I have learned, and been happy.'"

T. H. White, *The Once and Future King* (1958), pp.232-233, 234 (Kindle Edition, 2021).

Unfairness

It is frequently said that "life is unfair." I have certainly said it and have nodded agreement when others have. Curious, really. What does "unfair" mean in this context? Undeserved? For many people, most of the important things in his or her's life —good and bad—are undeserved. They are a matter of chance, of luck. Nothing you or your ancestors did or failed to do is responsible. (Of course, some things—good and bad—are deserved.)

Gleason writes:

"For me, I now believe the pain of this loss is fair. It's helped me learn to be resilient, forgiving, and compassionate. But, man, sometimes it doesn't seem fair to Gray and Rivers. Or even to Michel."

...

"It has become clear to me that experiencing stillness and silence have been my greatest adversaries, but mysteriously, my greatest teachers. Life is fair. Every breath, my prayer."

Gleason, pp.259-260, 277.

Reeve's reaction is certainly more typical:

"...[M]y deepest, almost overwhelming reaction was simply 'It's not fair.' Intellectually, I knew that life isn't fair and that bad things can happen to any of us at any time. Emotionally, I couldn't control myself. I demanded an answer to the apparently unanswerable question: Why me? What did I do to deserve this? It's not fair."

Reeve, p.159.

Actually, I cannot figure out what Gleason means about life being "fair" to him, but I can appreciate that it is unfair to his children and wife. Fairness is a relevant concept in connection with human institutions and human relationships. The chance things that happen to you are neither fair nor unfair to you, but they may have effects on others that, because of their relationships with you, are fairly labelled unfair.

Life itself is neither fair or unfair. It just is what it is.

Too rational? Perhaps.

But, we all face constraints and limitations that fate has imposed on us. Our height, our physical appearance, our athletic ability, our eyesight, our family, our race. We learn to live with what we are given. (Well, not all of us. Some struggle to alter and improve what nature provided.) Living with one's circumstances does not foreclose ambition or aspirations. We can make the best of what we got, changing what we can. Or, not, of course.

Life is full of wonders, of wonderous things. What matters is not how life treats us, but how we treat life. The human spirit can embrace and display passions, courage, dignity and reverence. What matters is how we respond to the joys and the tragedies, to the opportunities and the adversities.

Heroes

Are there still heroes?

Always. They may not be conspicuous. Most are like Dorothea, the heroine of *Middlemarch*.

"Her full nature ... spent itself in channels which had no great name on the earth. But the effect of her being on those around her was incalculably diffusive: for the **growing good of the world is partly dependent on unhistoric acts**; and that things are not so ill with you and me as they might have been, is **half owing to the number who lived faithfully a hidden life**, and rest in unvisited tombs."

George Eliot, *Middlemarch* (1872), Finale (emphasis added).

In the End

I fall back on, and embrace, quotations from two of my other favorite novels.

What is there in the end?

> "I believe that there is one story in the world, and only one.... . Humans are caught—in their lives, in their thoughts, in their hungers and ambitions, in their avarice and cruelty, and in their kindness and generosity too—in a net of good and evil. ... A man, after he has brushed off the dust and chips of his life, will have left only the hard clean questions: Was it good or was it evil? Have I done well—or ill?"

John Steinbeck, *East of Eden* (1952), pp.582.

And,

> "He was only a man who had meant well.... . Justice had been his last attempt—to do nothing which was not just. But it had ended in failure. To do at all had proved too difficult. He was done himself.

> "Arthur proved that he was not quite done, by lifting his head. There was something invincible in his heart, a tincture of grandness in simplicity. He sat upright and reached for the iron bell."

...

'"The cannons of his adversary were thundering in the tattered morning when the Majesty of England drew himself up to meet the future with a peaceful heart."

T. H. White, *The Once and Future King*, pp.819, 825.

"Have I done well ... ?"

ABOUT THE AUTHOR

John majored in economics at Amherst College, receiving a BA in 1970. He received his JD from The Harvard Law School in 1973. Following law school, he did post-graduate research at Trinity College, University of Cambridge. In late 1974, John began a 37-year career as a commercial litigator with a major law firm in New York City. He retired from the practice of law in 2011, after which he relocated to a small village outside of Cambridge, England. In March 2015, however, John was diagnosed with ALS (motor neuron disease). As a result, he decided to return to the U.S., to live in Old Town Alexandria, Virginia, with his daughter Sarah. His son John Eliot and daughter-in-law Megan, with his two grandchildren Hannah and Jeffrey, live nearby.

Confined to a wheelchair since 2018, he has been writing.

Books

Important Things We Don't Know (About Nearly Everting)
Wanderings of a Captive Mind (Wanderings Part 1)
The Eyes Have It (Wanderings Part 2)
All that Is Gold (Wanderings Part 3)
On Living While Dying: A Decade with ALS
Still Wandering: Still Wondering (Wanderings Part 4)
Politics, History and Ideology: Fruit of Forced Idleness
An Addendum to Important Things
Disappointments (Wanderings Part 5)

Milton Keynes UK
Ingram Content Group UK Ltd.
UKHW050929160624
443979UK00008B/108